Selections from

THE

ARCHITECTURAL HISTORY

OF THE

UNIVERSITY OF CAMBRIDGE

PETERHOUSE

THE

ARCHITECTURAL HISTORY

OF THE

UNIVERSITY OF CAMBRIDGE

AND OF THE

COLLEGES OF CAMBRIDGE

AND **ETON**

BY THE LATE
ROBERT WILLIS, M.A., F.R.S.

EDITED WITH LARGE ADDITIONS BY
JOHN WILLIS CLARK, M.A.

PETERHOUSE

CAMBRIDGE UNIVERSITY PRESS
Cambridge, New York, Melbourne, Madrid, Cape Town, Singapore, São Paulo, Delhi

Cambridge University Press
The Edinburgh Building, Cambridge CB2 8RU, UK

Published in the United States of America by Cambridge University Press, New York

www.cambridge.org
Information on this title: www.cambridge.org/9780521147149

First published 1886
This digitally printed version 2009

A catalogue record for this publication is available from the British Library

ISBN 978-0-521-14714-9 paperback

Peterhouse

Introduction by David Watkin

Though its buildings are not extensive or imposing, Peterhouse is important as the first college founded in Cambridge; it also has a Hall which is the earliest collegiate structure in the university. The origins of the college date to 1280 when Hugh de Balsham, a Benedictine monk and Bishop of the monastic cathedral of Ely, sought, as he put it, 'to introduce into the dwelling place of the secular brethren of his Hospital of St John [at Cambridge] studious scholars living according to the rule of the scholars of Oxford called of Merton.' Founded by Walter de Merton in 1264, Merton College was a religious community living under a rule with echoes of that of the Benedictine order as established by St Benedict, but devoted not primarily to prayer but to learning.

Finding the intrusion of de Balsham's scholars unwelcome, they and the scholars jointly appealed to him for a separation. In 1284, he accordingly removed the scholars to two Hostels in what is now Trumpington Street adjacent to the church of St Peter, now Little St Mary's. Providing the society with endowments, he effectively established it as a college, leaving it books, vestments, and 300 marks on his death in 1286. By 1339, it consisted of a Master and fourteen Fellows and was on the way to being self-governing, self-recruiting, and property-owning, the three conditions which guarantee the independence of the colleges of Oxford and Cambridge.

With its founder's 300 marks, the college acquired much of the land on which most of its future buildings stood, a process which doubtless began shortly after 1286 with the Hall. This was initially a free-standing structure, as it was at Merton College where the court was random in plan, rather than coherent. Old Court at Peterhouse was not formed until the fifteenth century when its surviving north and west ranges were built. The newel staircase to the former library on its west side is documented as the work in 1438-9 of Reginald Ely, one of the most outstanding architects of the century, and first master mason of King's College Chapel.

After the Hall, the most striking single building in the college is the Chapel, built in 1628-32 in a hybrid Gothic and Renaissance style promoted by the Master, Matthew Wren, uncle of the architect Sir Christopher Wren. Its unusual position in the middle of one side of the court, connected to the side ranges by galleries over cloister walks, doubtless influenced the arrangement of Wren's chapel at Emmanuel College of 1668-73. Matthew Wren had close connections with Charles I, and the superb stained glass Crucifixion of c.1630 in the east window of his Chapel at Peterhouse is based on a painting by Sir Peter Paul Rubens, knighted by Charles I in 1629. Wren would have added lasting fame to the college had he chosen Inigo Jones, Surveyor of the King's Works, to design the Chapel, though its Gothic elements may reflect the ideals of the High Church party under Archbishop Laud. Indeed, the Chapel was praised by the Gothic Revivalist, A.W.N. Pugin, in his Apology for the Revival of Christian Architecture in England (1843), as a building 'where many of the old principles were retained.'

In 1702, a Fellow who was son of a former Master, Dr Joseph Beaumont, built himself a substantial house in Trumpington Street opposite the college. By his will of 1725 he left this dignified Queen Anne mansion of red brick to the college to serve as the Master's Lodge, a role it continues to fill. In 1736, Sir James Burrough, a distinguished amateur architect and later Master of Gonville and Caius College, designed an elegant range of Fellows' chambers on the north side of the Chapel. Built in 1738-42, this much simplified version of Palladio's Palazzo Iseppo Porto in Vicenza, is known as Burrough's Building. In 1754-6 Burrough refaced with neat ashlar the façades of Old Court, inserting Georgian sash windows, as he had already done at Trinity Hall and at Gonville and Caius College where the mediaeval clunch had similarly decayed.

The Hall at Peterhouse was also Georgianised but was sympathetically restored and re-mediaevalised in 1867-70 by the architect George

Gilbert Scott, junior, with superb Pre-Raphaelite stained glass by Morris, Marshall, Faulkner & Co. The stencilling on the walls, probably dating from this time or perhaps marking the sexcentenary of the college in 1884, has diaper patterns recreating something of the effect of the tapestry which hung here till at least the late sixteenth century.

PROFESSOR DAVID WATKIN
Emeritus Professor of the History of Architecture
University of Cambridge
May 2009

INSATIABILITER DEFLEVIMUS, AETERNUMQUE

NULLA DIES NOBIS MOEROREM E PECTORE DEMET.

CONTENTS

PETERHOUSE.

LIST OF ILLUSTRATIONS

PREFACE.

THE work now published originated in a lecture *On the collegiate and other buildings in Cambridge*, delivered by Professor Willis in the Senate-House, on Wednesday, 5 July, 1854, on the occasion of the visit of the Archæological Institute of Great Britain and Ireland to Cambridge.

It would, however, be a mistake to suppose that he was then approaching the subject for the first time. When collecting materials for his *Architectural Nomenclature of the Middle Ages*, published by the Cambridge Antiquarian Society in 1844, he found that the changes in detail and in general treatment observed in the collegiate structures could not be satisfactorily explained without an inquiry into the various dates at which those structures had been originally built, or additions made to them. This inquiry he then determined to undertake. The lecture, therefore, was only one stage in the development of an original idea.

The lecture itself, on a subject which could not fail to interest, especially when set forth with his rare power of exposition and admirable delivery, excited the greatest enthusiasm, and he was requested to publish it without delay. This he undertook to do, though, as was his habit, he had used neither manuscript nor notes, and had only the reports in local newspapers to assist him; for, strange to say, no London reporter took the trouble to do more than give the briefest notice of the lecture. Before long, however, he found that it would be impossible to do justice to the subject within the narrow limits of a pamphlet, and he announced his intention of developing his lecture into a detailed history. But in this extended labour he made but slow progress. I imagine that when he began to collect materials for the original lecture, he had not contemplated publication at all, and that the labour of going through the authorities a second time, though obviously indispensable, soon became irksome to him. He accomplished this task however, for several colleges, at least up to a certain point, as for instance, for Trinity College, where he was evidently fascinated by the interesting problem which the original arrangement of the site presented, and where the presence of his friend Dr Whewell no doubt stimulated him to special activity. The extent of his research there is shewn by the enormous mass of material which he had collected, and by the numerous plans of the site which he had made and rejected, but which he evidently thought worth preserving for future reference. At King's College also, where the site is of nearly equal interest, he had made similar collections. I conceive that immediately after the delivery of the lecture, excited by the interest which he had aroused, and urged by the representations of friends, he set to work with great energy, and an intention to fulfil his promise of publication at an early date. In December, 1854, in a letter to Mr C. H.

Cooper, the well-known Cambridge antiquary, he speaks of "the complete form of that paper which I am now preparing;" and in the same month the Master and Seniors of Trinity College agreed: "that Professor Willis have leave to publish such extracts from the Books and Documents of the College submitted to his inspection, as tend, in his opinion, to illustrate the Architectural History of the College and the University." Again, in 1856, he was at work on the records of Trinity Hall; and in 1860, when he gave a second lecture on *The Architectural History of the University*, on the occasion of the meeting of the Architectural Congress at Cambridge, he told his audience that "he purposed to bring out a book on the subject very shortly. He had hoped to have done so before this, but he had been under the necessity of deferring it. The work was now in the printer's hands, and he hoped ere long to throw it on their mercy." This second lecture shewed most conclusively the extent of his researches in the six years which had passed away since he had first approached the subject, and it was on that occasion that he first brought forward some of his most celebrated illustrations, as for instance, the comparison between the plans of Queens' College and Haddon Hall, the diagrams shewing the successive changes in the west front of Clare Hall, and the contrast between the aspect of Nevile's Court at Trinity College at the present day, and when it was first constructed. In the following year, as Sir Robert Rede's lecturer, he chose a portion of the subject for more minute illustration—lecturing in the Senate-House on *The Architectural History of Trinity College*. The

promise of speedy publication, however, was, as we all
know, never fulfilled, and I am surprised that he should
ever have made it in such definite terms. It was retarded by many causes: his natural unwillingness to
print before he felt himself thoroughly prepared; the
steady increase in the bulk of his materials as he went
on, which, as he told me more than once, grew so fast
that he felt at a loss how to treat them; doubts as to
the form of the work, and the means of defraying its
cost; the pressure of his official duties in Cambridge
and in London; the work which he undertook in connection with the exhibition held at Paris in 1855; and
lastly, his continued devotion to the interests of the
Archæological Institute, which carried him away to
Gloucester (1860), Peterborough (1861), Worcester (1862),
Rochester (1863), Lichfield (1864), Sherborne and Glas-
tonbury (1865), and Eton (1866), for all of which meet-
ings he prepared papers of considerable length, involving a corresponding amount of research.

In 1869—when he had resigned his Professorship
at the Royal School of Mines—his friends at Cambridge
hoped to induce him to resume the work which appeared to have been definitely laid aside, and, through
the combined influence of Dr Guest, Master of Gonville
and Caius College, and Dr Atkinson, Master of Clare
College, then Vice-Chancellor, he was induced to write
the following letter :

"Dear Mr Vice-Chancellor,

I beg to inform you that having resigned my office of
Lecturer on Mechanism at the School of Mines I am at leisure to
complete a work, which I began many years since, on the Architectural
and Social History of the University of Cambridge.

As this is a work involving considerable expense in production, and not likely to command a remunerative sale, I have been advised to ask you whether you think the Press Syndicate would be willing to assist in any way towards the publication of the work.

The greater part of it is prepared for the press, and, should your opinion be favourable, I would immediately resume the preparation of the work for the press.

The Rede lecture which I had the honor of delivering in 1861 in the presence of the Prince Consort may be taken as a fair specimen of the manner in which the History of the University and all the Colleges is treated in my work.

I remain,

Dear Mr Vice-Chancellor,

Yours most truly,

R. WILLIS."

CAMBRIDGE,
June 4, 1869.

The Syndics of the University Press intimated without delay their willingness to give every assistance in their power, as soon as a tolerably accurate statement of the extent of the work, and the quantity of illustrations required for it, should be placed before them; and, a few days later, a memorial, signed by eleven Heads of Colleges, and forty-two Members of the Senate, respectfully requested Professor Willis "to publish the materials which he has collected for elucidating the history of the Collegiate Structures in Cambridge, and to allow their names to appear as subscribers to the proposed work."

This expression of interest gave him much satisfaction, and he unquestionably intended to resume and complete his work; but, before doing so, he felt himself under an obligation to Messrs Longman to prepare a new edition of his *Principles of Mechanism*, then out of print; and, when this obstacle was removed, the illness and death of Mrs Willis gave a shock to his system from which he never recovered sufficiently to resume any literary work whatever. He often spoke of his Cambridge book, and used occasionally to take out the manuscript and read it, but he was so much enfeebled that he could not even superintend its completion by others. At the same time, though he told me that he had bequeathed the manuscript and all the materials to me, he was unwilling to part with it during his lifetime. He died on Sunday, 28 February, 1875.

When I first examined the manuscript, which was neatly written out, and sorted in folios marked with the names of the different subjects treated of, it appeared to be much more nearly finished than it ultimately proved to be; and I thought that my task would be limited to the verification of references, and the selection of subjects for illustration. I soon found, however, that I had fallen into a grievous error. At no college was the work quite finished; if the history of the buildings was complete, that of the site would be unfinished, or vice versâ. At King's College for instance the history of the chapel had hardly been begun, though that of the site had been carefully investigated; at S. John's College the entire history was unfinished, which was the more to be regretted, as it was known that Professor Willis had carefully watched the destruction of the old chapel in 1869, and had made notes upon it; while even at Trinity College, though the history of the site, and of King's Hall, had been written out at length, that of the buildings was by no means complete. Everywhere, in fact, there were gaps to be

filled up, but no materials suitable for the purpose were
at hand. Notes and sketches existed in abundance,
but the greater part of them were written in a species
of shorthand, to which he alone could have supplied
the key. Under these circumstances I came to the
conclusion that in order to produce the work in a way
which should be worthy alike of the author and of the
University, it would be necessary to go back to the
point from which he had himself started, and investi-
gate the whole subject afresh. When this had been
done, and not till then, I felt that I should be in a
position to edit what he had already prepared, and to
complete those portions which he had left unfinished.
The necessity for this comprehensive and thorough
research will, it is hoped, give a satisfactory explana-
tion of the length of time, just eleven years, which has
passed away since I began my work. I have read,
and made extracts from, the entire series of bursars'
account-books for every college in the University, besides studying the documents relating to the history
of the sites, the Order-books, and all other sources of
information to which I could obtain access, both at
Cambridge and elsewhere. A similar labour has been
required for the University buildings. These records,
especially those of the fourteenth and fifteenth centuries, as for instance the accounts of King's Hall, and
those of the Proctors of the University, are exceedingly
difficult to read, and require a good deal of prelimi-
nary study before any extracts of value can be made
from them. Severe as this labour has been, I cannot
regret it; for these volumes supply a detailed record
of the life of our ancestors, from which, as will be

seen in the separate essays, a complete picture of their manners and customs at different periods can be derived.

Eton College has been included in the work, at my suggestion, partly on account of its close connection with King's College, and partly because the lecture in which Professor Willis set forth its architectural history in 1866—the last, it may be added, which he ever delivered -was considered to be more than usually brilliant and original. But the causes which stood in the way of the completion of his larger work, prevented him from even attempting to prepare this essay for publication. The materials with which I had to deal were in this case more than usually scanty. The introduction only to the lecture had been written, and this dealt with matters of general interest, of no use for the architectural history of Eton College, while the building-accounts, and the bursars' accounts, which are remarkably voluminous and interesting, had been but imperfectly examined. The lecture, again, had been reported with provoking brevity ; in fact, the only record of the conclusions at which he had arrived is contained in three columns of *The Athenæum*. This brief summary, with the correctness of which he appears to have been satisfied, as he had carefully preserved it, will be found at the end of this Preface. I have taken it as the basis of my attempt to write such an essay as he would have wished to see ; and it will be found that my conclusions, after a far more extended study of the authorities than he had had leisure for, do not clash in any way with his. This part of my work, agreeable as it has been to me, from the affection which I naturally feel towards the school at which I was educated, and from the great interest attaching to the subject, has necessitated a larger expenditure of time, thought, and labour, than any other.

The general arrangement of the whole work had fortunately been carefully considered by Professor Willis, and he had drawn up for his own use the following scheme:

CONTENTS.

A. History.	General chronological History of the Colleges (add motives and special purposes). College and Hall. History of name. Socii and scholares. Perendinants, pensioners, tutors. Studies and Teachers. Servants. Statutes.
B. Architecture and general arrangement of the separate buildings. Sites.	Separate Architectural History of each College, and of the University Buildings, from the beginning to the present time, including the history of each site. Chronological summary.
C. Special arrangement of each building.	General plan of a College. Chapels. Chambers, Studies, and other fittings; number of persons in each, and their classification. Hall, Kitchen, Combination Room, Lodge, Library, Gates, Treasury.
D. University Buildings.	University Schools. Senate House. Lecture Rooms. Contracts.

This scheme could be followed in its general outline without difficulty, but for separate details I have often had to content myself with the indication afforded by a single line, or an unfinished sketch. For instance, in the essay on *The Library*, the following passage occurs : "At the beginning of this century, however, in the time of Queen Elizabeth, the Library of Trinity Hall was built and fitted with desks which still remain, and are furnished with a complete mechanism for chaining the books. This is the only example that I have been able to discover in Cambridge, and it is so curious that I proceed to describe it at length"; but the rest of the page is blank. These words, however, shewed me that my uncle had intended to deal with the medieval system of chaining books, and I have therefore done my best to work out the whole subject, as part of the history of library-fittings in general, for which he had left copious notes. His interest in woodwork is well known, and I hope that this essay will be found to be one of the most valuable, and at the same time popular, of the series. In other essays, I regret to say, completion has not been easy, and, in some, not even possible. In that on *The Gateway*, the whole subject of the wooden doors, with which the gateways were originally closed, has been of necessity omitted, because the materials to my hand were so fragmentary that it was impossible to ascertain how he had proposed to treat the subject, as I have explained in the text (Vol. III. p. 295); and the essay on *The Style of Collegiate Buildings*, which he had intended to turn into a history of the influence of the Renaissance on Architecture, has been left, for the same reason, in a wretchedly attenuated condition. In all my additions—and it will be seen that they extend to nearly two-thirds of the whole work in its present form—I

have strictly confined myself within the limits which
the author had traced for his own guidance; remem-
bering at the same time that he proposed to write
not merely "the architectural" history, but "the architectural and social" history; by which epithets I understand that the modifications introduced into collegiate
structures by the changing habits of those who use
them are always to be borne in mind and noticed. I
can only hope that I shall not be thought to have deve-
loped this part of my subject, which, as possessing a
human interest, is naturally the most fascinating, with
too great minuteness. All added matter has been distinguished by enclosure within square brackets.

I am not merely employing a conventional figure of
speech when I say that I wish that some other person
than myself had been selected to edit and complete so important a work as this. Archæology, like other sciences,
especially in these days, when all knowledge is so highly
specialised, demands a regular and definite training from
those who aim at professing it, and my time, until this
task was thrust upon me, had been fully occupied with
other and wholly different pursuits. Hence I am afraid
that the architectural portion of the work will have
suffered through my inexperience, while in that which
is strictly editorial I am conscious of numerous defects,
more especially in the histories of the earlier colleges,
which were finished before I had fully realised the best
method of sorting and arranging the materials presented
to me. My anxiety to leave untouched what Professor
Willis had written, whenever it was possible to do so,
led me too frequently to forget that the work had not
received his final revision, and that one of the clearest

of writers would have been specially careful to avoid confusion. Further, I have to apologise for a certain want of uniformity between the earlier and later volumes, chiefly in the spelling of proper names. This has arisen, in the main, from the unexpected length to which the work has extended, so that the earlier portions had to be printed off before the later portions were begun.

In preparing some of the more important illustrations of existing buildings, and parts of buildings, I have had the advantage of the artistic talent of my friend John O'Connor, Esq. I wish to draw attention to the beautiful views of Queens' College, of the Fountain and Nevile's Gate at Trinity College, and of the Bath at Christ's College, all of which are by him. The reproductions of the celebrated series of prints by David Loggan, the appearance of which will be considered, I imagine, to be a novel and interesting feature of the work, were, for the most part, executed, like the rest of the wood-engravings, by Mr F. Anderson, to whom my best thanks are due, not only for his professional skill, but for his courtesy in deferring to my wishes on all occasions.

The plans of the colleges have, as a general rule, been based on those prepared in connection with the Award Act of 1856, tested by actual measurements, and brought up to date. In this matter, however, where exact uniformity was not necessary, the plan of each college has been treated with reference to the particular case. In some, as at Trinity Hall and Emmanuel College, older plans have been reproduced; in others, as at Peterhouse and Eton College, entirely original surveys have been prepared. The plan of the buildings of Trinity College is based upon one measured and drawn by Professor Willis before the Award Act plans were made ; and those of the ground floor and first floor of the Schools Quadrangle were measured and drawn by myself. For some of the older colleges, where it seemed desirable to exhibit the original and the existing arrangements together, the former have been drawn on paper, and the latter on tracing-linen placed above it. This device was suggested by a work, called *Paris à travers les Ages*, published in parts by Messrs Hachette between 1875 and 1882.

A research such as I have had to undertake depended for its success upon the cooperation of all who have the charge of University and College records. From all these, both here, at Oxford, and at the British Museum and Public Record Office, London, I have experienced unvaried kindness, and I beg them to accept this collective expression of my gratitude. In addition to these, however, there are some to whom I am under such particular obligations, that I wish to mention them by name.

My warmest thanks are due, in the first place, to the Reverend D. J. Stewart, M.A., of Trinity College, one of her Majesty's Inspectors of Schools. Mr Stewart, himself an accomplished archæologist and skilful artist, was an intimate friend of Professor Willis, frequently assisting him in the examination and measurement of buildings, and in discussing with him the arrangement of his work on Cambridge. His help has therefore been of peculiar value to me, as it has enabled me to ascertain, in numerous doubtful cases, what method my uncle intended to have followed, had he been able to prepare his own work for press. Mr Stewart not only placed all his notes at my disposal in the kindest manner, and allowed me to consult him at all times since my work began, but has been at the trouble of reading the greater part of the proof-sheets, thereby saving me from many errors into which I should otherwise have fallen. The value of this help has been most conspicuous in the history of Jesus College Chapel, and in that of S. Benedict's Church.

I have also to acknowledge the help which I received from two friends, now, I regret to say, no more, the Reverend J. Lamb, M.A., Fellow of Gonville and Caius College; and the Reverend C. J. Evans, M.A., Fellow of King's College. The former added valuable notes to the history of his own college; the latter contributed the important essay on the Heraldry of King's College Chapel. Besides these, the Reverend G. F. Browne, B.D., formerly Fellow of S. Catharine's College, most kindly placed at my disposal the collections he had formed for the history of his college, and made valuable criticisms on my work; Professor C. C. Babington, M.A., of S. John's College, gave me much help in preparing the history of his own college, and, further, allowed me to use the illustrations which had been prepared for his own work on the old chapel, besides illustrations for other parts of the book; the accurate ground-plan of King's College Chapel, the plan of the Conference Chamber at Jesus College, and the section of the Gallery at Queens' College, were made for me by my friend W. H. St John Hope, M.A., of Peterhouse, now Secretary to the Society of Antiquaries;

the heraldry of Trinity College Library, and of Magdalene College Chapel, were contributed by L. H. Cust, M.A., of Trinity College; and much help in preparing the index was given by F. R. Pryor, B.A., of Trinity College.

I am also much indebted to the Warden and Fellows of All Souls College, Oxford, for allowing me to copy Sir C. Wren's designs for Trinity College library; to Mr H. Maxwell Lyte, and to Messrs Macmillan, for the use of a large number of the beautiful illustrations which had already appeared in Mr Lyte's *History of Eton College;* to Messrs Metcalfe, booksellers, of Cambridge, for a similar permission with regard to several line engravings, previously used in the late Mr C. H. Cooper's edition of Le Keux's *Memorials of Cambridge;* and to the proprietors of *The Portfolio* for the gift of a woodcut of the façade of the Pepysian Library at Magdalene College, and of two woodcuts of buildings of S. John's College.

I have reserved to the last the name of the dear friend to whom I am under deeper obligations than I can put into words. No language that I can think of can adequately express what I owe to our late Librarian, Henry Bradshaw, M.A., Senior Fellow of King's College. From the outset of my work he took it, so to speak, into his hands, and treated it as if it had been his own. Notwithstanding the incessant demands upon his time, he always found leisure to help me, to teach me to read difficult medieval handwriting, or to dictate to me some document which I had occasion to copy. On one occasion, I remember, he took the trouble to travel from Cambridge to Eton in order to settle the signification of a single contraction in one of the building-rolls, on which a good deal depended, and about which I could not feel quite sure.   Not content with giving me advice on all questions of arrangement of materials—about which his singularly lucid and orderly mind rendered him an invaluable counsellor—he insisted on reading all the proof-sheets—not merely for the purpose of detecting clerical errors, but that he might copiously annotate them, and shew me how difficult points in history and archæology might be set in the best light.   Had it not been for his encouragement, my labours would never have been brought to a conclusion.   My greatest pleasure would have been to shew him the completed work; my greatest grief is that he can never see it.

In conclusion, I wish to express my gratitude to the Syndics of the University Press, for the splendid liberality with which they have published the work, and for the patience with which they have submitted to the long, and wholly unexpected, delay, by which its production has been retarded.   Nor can I allow it to pass out of my hands without thanking the staff of the Press, not only for the anxiety they have shewn to produce it in the best possible manner, but for many acts of personal kindness to myself.

JOHN WILLIS CLARK.

Scroope House, Cambridge,
21 *April*, 1886.

APPENDIX.

Report of the Lecture delivered by Professor Willis before the Archæological Institute at Eton, August, 1866; from *The Athenæum* for 4 August, 1866.

PROF. WILLIS ON THE ARCHITECTURAL HISTORY OF THE COLLEGE AT ETON.

"The Professor prefaced his account with some introductory remarks on the general history of colleges and their growth. The universities were at first corporations of educated men, the teachers or doctors in which instructed by lectures in the public schools, the students being obliged to find lodgings for themselves. Soon, however, generous persons gave funds to assist poor students. After a time a more definite shape was assumed by these institutions; and lodgings were also provided, that the morals and manners of these students might be brought under superintendence and control. The next step was to purchase houses, endow them and provide them with statutes. Thus arose the communities termed colleges, residing in buildings called the *Domus* or *Aula*, which at first contained little else than chambers to lodge in, with a dining-hall, kitchen, &c., like the ordinary dwelling-house of the period. The first of these colleges was that at Oxford, by Walter de Merton, in 1264; one was founded at Cambridge soon after; and others followed at intervals up to 1379, when in the so-called New College at Oxford William of Wykeham erected the first architectural building, complete in all its details, and so well organized in its statutes, as well as in its structures, as to serve as a basis for all subsequent erections. His plans also included the then new feature of a preparatory school, at Winchester, for young boys, from whom the members of his Oxford College were to be selected.—The Professor next proceeded to the consideration of King's College, Cambridge, and its appendage Eton. He gave a touching account of the effect of the misfortunes of Henry the Sixth in retarding and finally suspending these works, followed by a just parallel between the continual devising of plans for the education and elevation of his people by that monarch and the constant efforts in the same directions by the late Prince Consort.—Prof. Willis then detailed the original plans for Eton College as set forth in that monarch's 'will'—this will being, however, not a 'last will and testament,' but in reality a building specification for his colleges, in which so clearly has he laid down his plans that the lecturer was able to transfer them to paper, and to exhibit diagrams of the ground-plans to his audience as a basis for comparison with a plan prepared by himself of the actual buildings subsequently erected, and shewing the condition of Eton in 1866. Henry, however, did not mature his plans at once, but modified them very considerably

at a shortly subsequent period.   He first founded a collegiate grammar-
school at Eton and a small college at Cambridge, dedicated to St Nicholas,
that saint's day having been his birthday.   A site was purchased at
Eton, north of the cemetery of the old parish church (now no more), and
the King came down and laid the first stone, over which was to be the
high altar of the new collegiate church.   The King soon enlarged
his plans, increasing the number of his beneficiaries and connecting, by
statutes copied from Wykeham's, Eton School with King's College at
Cambridge.

The contemporary building accounts and documents, containing
the King's projects and instructions, long mislaid, and believed to have
been stolen, were by a fortunate accident discovered in a forgotten
recess of the Library at Eton, about two months since, and liberally
submitted to the Professor's inspection.   They contain abundant proofs
of the personal interest which the King took in the details of the
college buildings, and of changes and improvements introduced by him
as time went on.   They shew that the works at Eton were of two kinds,
carried on simultaneously.   First, the enlarging, refitting, and altering
of buildings that already stood on the site purchased by the King,
including the parish church, of which he obtained the advowson, and
its conversion into a collegiate church.   These buildings were so treated
as to make them serve as temporary dwellings for the accommodation
of the provost, fellows, and students of his new College, which enabled
the school to be brought into active existence from the beginning,
without waiting for the erection of the magnificent architectural pile
described in his will and other documents, and which was commenced
simultaneously with these temporary operations; but which, even if
carried on in prosperous times, would necessarily have occupied many
years in completion.   The chancel of the old parish church was rebuilt
on a larger scale, and fitted with stalls and other appurtenances for the
daily choral service.   A hall in one of the old houses was enlarged;
a school-room and other buildings constructed of wood.   The alms-
house for poor men, described in the will, was also built.

The permanent College was also begun; the first buildings attacked
being the great chapel, which now exists, and the hall and kitchens.
This chapel was placed in the old parish church-yard, to the north of the
old parish church, and was planned as the chancel of a large collegiate
church, to be provided with a nave or body for the parishioners, as
described in the well-known will of Henry the Sixth, dated 1448.   But,
after the signature of this will, the King enlarged and altered his plans.
He sent persons to Sarum and Winton, and other parts, to measure the
choirs and naves of churches there, and had improved designs made for
the college buildings.

The Professor found among the documents two specifications relating
to the chapel, the one exactly corresponding to that of the will, but in
which every dimension is struck through with a pen, and an increased
dimension written above it.   The other specification describes the chapel
or church, as it is called, in different phraseology from that of the will,
and more completely.   The dimensions in this latter paper are still
greater than those of the corrected document, and, what is more

curious still, they correspond exactly with the chapel as it exists. The paper concludes with minute directions that the foundations of the chapel, which had already been laid (of course in accordance with the will, for the works had been in progress for seven years before that will was signed), should not be disturbed, but the new foundations (i.e. for the enlarged dimensions) be laid round the outside of them, and be constructed with the greatest care, and with 'mighty mortar.' The first stone under the high altar to remain undisturbed. This stone was protected by a small chapel built over it in the first years of the works.

The deposition of the King, in 1461, put an abrupt stop to the buildings, which had languished during his increasing misfortunes. That they were resumed, after a long interval of time, by his confidential friend and executor Bishop Waynflete, is stated by Leland, and also shewn by an indenture, in 1475, between him and a carver, who engaged to make a roodloft and stalls for the new chapel, and to take down the roodloft and stalls in the choir of the old parish church. This proves that the great chapel was only then brought into a condition to receive its fittings. It must have been just roofed in. The Professor pointed out to his audience evidences of the haste in which the upper part of the chapel had been completed. The arch heads of the windows are abruptly depressed, in a way which shews that the walls of the chapel were intended to have been carried much higher by the masons who built the jambs and springing of the window-arches. It is probable that the work had been carried up exactly to this level when the defeat of the King stopped the operations. When resumed by Waynflete, with insufficient funds, expedients were adopted to enable the buildings to be rapidly finished and roofed-in for use. The hall exhibits similar evidences to shew that its walls and windows were designed to have been carried up to a much greater elevation than they now present; and that after a sudden interruption it had been hastily put into a condition to receive the roof, which is of a very plain construction. The magnificent body of the collegiate church designed by the founder was never even commenced. The choir, or present chapel, is now terminated westward by a low transverse ante-chapel of slight construction, probably the work of Waynflete.

The old parish church appears to have been pulled down after the present chapel was prepared for service, as above stated. The parishioners retained the right of employing this chapel as their parish church. But the increase in the numbers of the students and of the population, and other causes, creating great inconvenience, both to the college and the parish, a new church or chapel-of-ease was erected in the town of Eton for the use of the parishioners, in the last century.

The arrangement of the college buildings differs entirely from that described in the will of the founder in 1448. The Professor concluded from this, and from the mention of a plan or 'Portratura' exhibited to the King, in the following year, 'for the finishing of the buildings of the college,' that he, when adopting an enlarged design for the chapel, had also determined upon a new disposition for the other buildings.

The college in the will is imitated from Wykeham's colleges, consisting of a quadrangle containing hall, library and chambers, and of a cloister. But in the existing college the quadrangle of chambers contains not only the hall and library, but is also cloistered. The site of the cloister first proposed, but never commenced, is that now occupied by the school-yard. The cloister quadrangle is arranged upon a plan unusual in colleges. It was built in two stories, having chambers on the north and east sides, and the hall on the south, the dimensions of which agree exactly with the founder's will. The upper chambers are not reached in the usual manner, by assigning one staircase to each contiguous pair; but a gallery is carried round the upper floor, exactly over the cloister of the ground floor, to give access to the doors of the chambers. At each internal angle of the quadrangle, or *quadrant*, as the will terms it, is a square turret containing a spiral stone stair, or *vice*, with a door below and above, by which the upper gallery is conveniently reached.

The chamber buildings were carried round the east and north sides in one style, and probably in the founder's time; but the west side, which contains the great gateway called Lupton's Tower, was built, after a considerable pause in the works, in a totally different manner, during the provostship of [Roger] Lupton [1504—35], and probably in the reign of Henry the Eighth.

The cloister-arcade and chamber-doors on the ground floor on this side appear, however, to belong to the earlier building, and to have been suddenly stopped in an unfinished state. This western side of the quadrant is wholly devoted to the provost, and contains a large dining-hall, termed 'Election Hall,' with a withdrawing-room behind it, over Lupton's entrance-arch, and large bedchambers beyond, joining the hall. In the will of the founder a much smaller provost's lodging is placed in this position in two stories. The present extension is accounted for by the bountiful hospitality which, at and after the period of Henry the Eighth, was exercised by the masters of colleges in favour of the nobility and gentry. This compelled the building of chambers and reception-rooms. After the Reformation the marriage of masters of colleges created a new demand for space, and made it necessary to supply these officers with a family residence.

The subsequent works carried out in this college were enumerated as follows: The lower school, or north side of the entrance quadrangle or 'school-yard,' was built before 1581 [1481?], and has the long dormitory above it. The library in the cloister quadrangle was built by Sir Christopher Wren[1]. The new upper school, which is the western boundary of the school-yard, was rebuilt in 1689. In 1758 an attic was raised upon the east and north sides of the cloister court, and the entire group of chambers altered so as to convert them into a row of private houses of three stories each for the fellows of the college. Lastly, the interior of the chapel, which had been refitted and 'beautified' in the Italian style in 1699, by Mr Banks, was well restored to its ancient aspect, with rich stalls and canopies, in 1850, from the designs of Mr Deason."

[1] [This is a mistake. Sir C. Wren died in 1723, and the library was not begun until 1725 (Vol. I. p. 455).]

Peterhouse. Plan showing changes and additions, 1641 - 1825

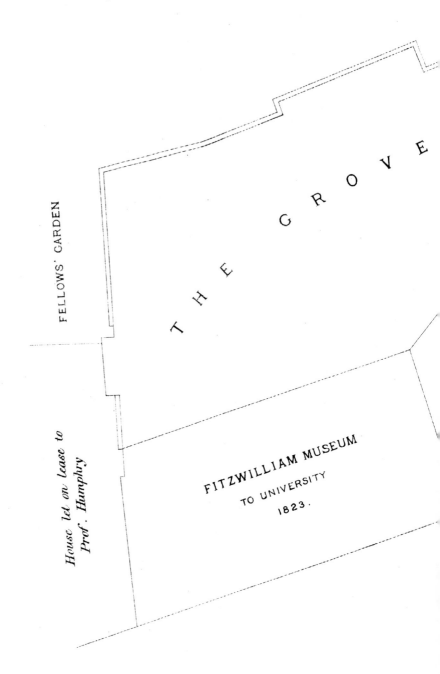

FELLOWS' GARDEN

THE GROVE

House let on lease to Prof. Humphry

FITZWILLIAM MUSEUM
TO UNIVERSITY
1823.

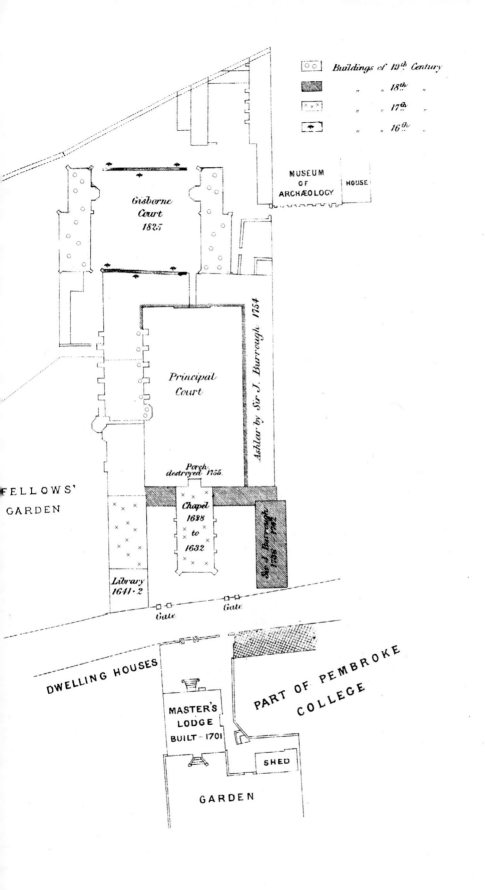

Buildings of 19th Century

    „ „ 18th „

    „ „ 17th „

    „ „ 16th „

MUSEUM
OF
ARCHÆOLOGY

HOUSE

Gisborne
Court
1825

Ashlar by Sir J. Burrough 1754

Principal
Court

Porch
destroyed 1755.

FELLOWS'
GARDEN

Chapel
1628
to
1632

Sir J. Burrough 1745

Library
1641·2

Gate

Gate

DWELLING HOUSES

PART OF PEMBROKE COLLEGE

MASTER'S
LODGE
BUILT — 1701

SHED

GARDEN

Plan of the History of Peterhouse

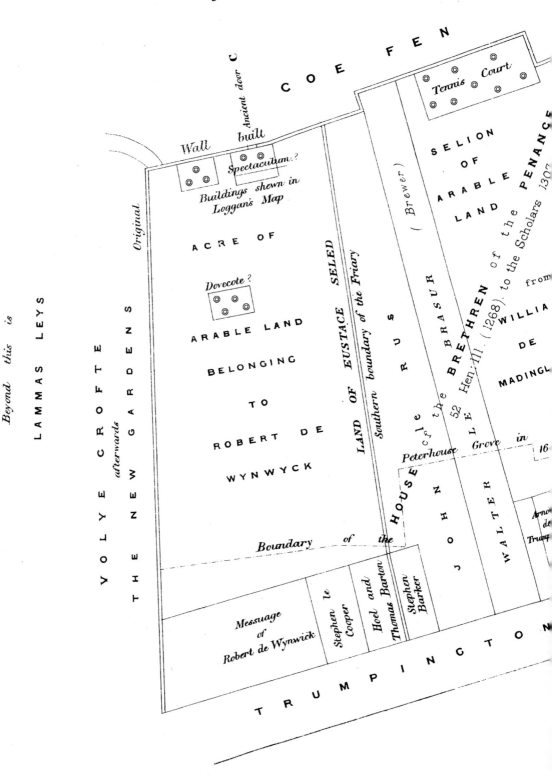

Beyond this is

LAMMAS LEYS

VOLYE CROFTE
afterwards

THE NEW GARDENS

Original

Wall built

Ancient door C

C O E   F E N

Spectaculum ?

Buildings shewn in
Loggan's Map

ACRE   OF

Dovecote ?

ARABLE   LAND

BELONGING

TO

ROBERT   DE

WYNWYCK

Boundary   of   the

Messuage
of
Robert de Wynwick

Stephen le
Cooper

Hoel and
Thomas Barton

Stephen
Barker

LAND OF EUSTACE SELED

Southern boundary of the Friary

(Brewer)

HOUSE of the BRASUR

LE   BRETHREN

52 Hen. III. (1268)

of the Scholars 1307

to the Scholars

from

WILLIA

DE

MADINGL

Peterhouse Grove in

16

J O H N

W A L T E R

Arno
de
Trum

SELION
OF
ARABLE
LAND PENANC

Tennis Court

T R U M P I N G T O N

1501-2

Ortus coci?

BOUGHT WITH DE BALSHAM'S

HUGH DE BALSHAM'S BEQUEST IN 1280

LAND

DWELLING HOUSES

CHURCHYARD OF S.MARY THE LESS

Kitchen

Buttery

Arbour

Hall

Comb.ⁿ Room with Lodge over

Library 1590

AYLSHAM

Entrance closed 1754

CHURCH OF S.MARY THE LESS.

LAND BELONGING TO THE CHAPEL OF S. EDMUND).

GARDEN ASSIGNED TO THE MASTER

PROPERTY OF RICHARD DE

The original Hostels and their Ground.

Messuage of Sabina widow of John de Aylsham

Dwelling House reserved

Chambers destroyed 1632, and rebuilt with Richardsons bequest taken down 1732

Entrance to Churchyard closed 1742

LITTLE S. MARY'S LANE

S   T   R   E   E   T

⊙⊙ Buildings of the 14ᵗʰ and
15ᵗʰ Centuries, conjectural
or otherwise.

SCALE, 80 FEET TO 1 INCH

0 10 20 30 40 50 60 70 80 90 100   150   200 Feet.

Plan of the Existing Buildings of Peterhouse

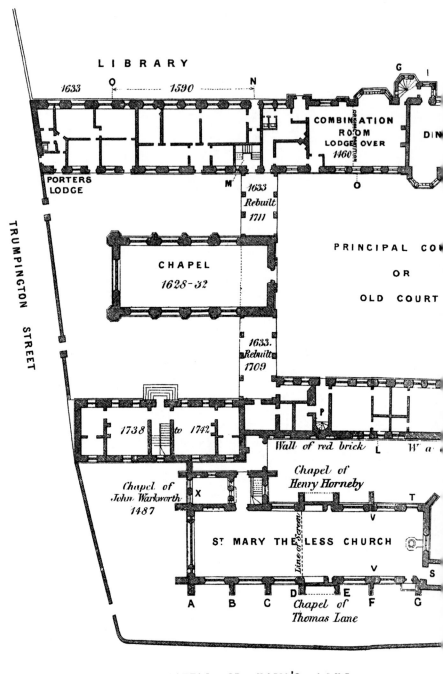

SCALE 40 FEET TO 1 INCH.

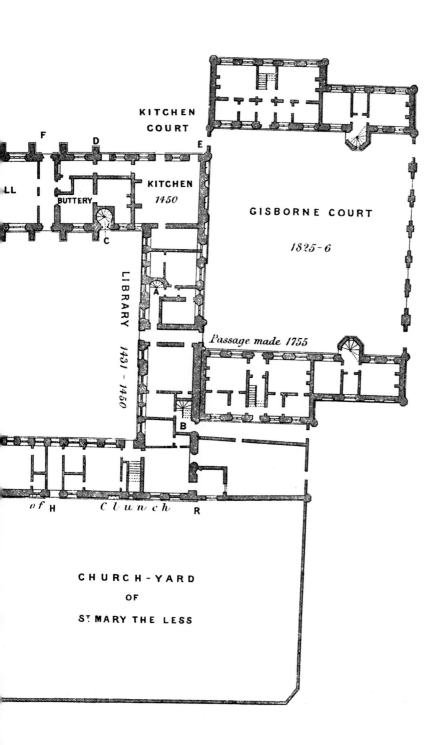

KITCHEN
COURT

F   D   E

LL

BUTTERY   KITCHEN
           1450

C

GISBORNE COURT

1825-6

LIBRARY

1431 - 1450

A

Passage made 1755

B

of H   *Clunch*   R

CHURCH-YARD

OF

S.ᵗ MARY THE LESS

I.

Peterhouse.

CHAPTER I.

[HISTORY OF THE SITE[1].

THE site of Peterhouse is bounded on the east by Trumpington Street; on the south by an estate bequeathed to Caius College by the Lady Ann Scroope, called Lammas Leys; on the west by Coe Fen; on the north by the churchyard of S. Mary the Less, anciently S. Peter, and by some dwelling-houses.

The southern portion of this extensive ground, anciently called "Volye Croft," and afterwards "English Croft," and "The New Gardens," originally belonged to the White Canons of S. Edmund of Sempringham, whose house, called "Chanons Close," was directly opposite to it on the east side of Trumpington Street[2]. Volye Croft was purchased by Peterhouse in the reign of Elizabeth, at which time it was laid out as a garden, and let on lease, the College reserving the right of entrance for recreation or exercise, and the tenant engaging to keep the walks "fair and passable and well graviled." In 1795 the eastern two-thirds were let on a building lease, as at present.

---

[1] [The accompanying map (fig. 1) has been drawn to illustrate this.]

[2] [Fuller, pp. 57, 67. The position of Chanons Close is shewn on the map of Ric. Lyne, 1574, for which see the History of Corpus Christi College below. The S. wall of the site of the Fitzwilliam Museum would fall nearly in a line with the N. wall of the Close, which has now become the site of Addenbrooke's Hospital.]

The rest of the site was originally included within the stone wall which still exists entire along the western boundary, and along the southern also, as far as the piece sold to the University in 1823 as a site for the Fitzwilliam Museum. Before that sale it probably extended to Trumpington Street (fig. 1), in which position a wall is shewn in the maps of Hammond (fig. 3) and of Loggan. The history of the ground within it, including that on which the College buildings stand, must now be investigated.

The materials for this are to be found in the original conveyances, which have been preserved in Peterhouse Treasury. From these it is tolerably easy to make out the relative positions of several of the parcels of ground described in them: but certain intermediate ones have been lost, so that it is impossible to draw up as complete a map of the site as can be done for some other Colleges[1]. A few particulars of interest may however be gleaned respecting it.

When the Founder, Bishop Hugh de Balsham, removed his scholars from the Hospital of S. John, he placed them in two hostels hard by the church of S. Peter without Trumpington gates[2]. The precise position of these edifices cannot now be determined, although they appear, from the College accounts, to have existed in name at least down to the beginning of the seventeenth century, when "the little ostle" was destroyed to

---

[1] [These documents had never been seen by Professor Willis. He had studied only the four that are to be found in the Old Register of Peterhouse, pp. 57, 8, out of which some earlier leaves, which doubtless contained the others, have unfortunately been torn. His history of the site was therefore of necessity most imperfect. I have in consequence cancelled the short account that he had drawn up, and substituted one which I have written after a careful study of the whole evidence. By the kindness of my friend the Rev. James Porter, the present Master, I have had every facility for examining these documents and also the Bursars' Rolls. Richard Parker, History, etc., p. 38, mentions a tradition that the archives of this house were destroyed by fire before 1420, which may account for the absence of some of the conveyances. Professor Willis remarks that Parker "never quotes authorities, but in this instance probably copied a note from an Ely Register."]

[2] [The date of the Bishop's acquisition of the Hostels is unknown, but the scholars were moved into them in the beginning of the year 1284, and the Royal charter, confirming the Bishop's acts, is dated May 28, 13 Edward I. (1285). Old Register of Peterhouse, p. 25. Commiss. Doc[ts]. ii. 1. For the facts relating to the foundation see Historical Introduction.]

make way for the chapel. Hammond's map (fig. 3) shews a narrow range of building close to the street along the east side of the entrance court and projecting beyond the present Library to the south. As most of the houses on this part of the site consisted of small messuages abutting on the street, with large gardens behind them extending to the fen ("usque ad mariscum"), it is quite possible that this range of building may represent, in part at least, the original hostels. Some quaint old houses next to the Library (fig. 4), which may be regarded as representing the southern end of the range, were not pulled down until 1841[1].

When the Bishop was on his death-bed, he bequeathed to his scholars 300 marks, "with which they bought a certain area to the south of the Church, and built thereon a handsome Hall[2]." As he died on June 16, 1286, the date of this acquisition can be fixed within a few years: and as the present Hall will be shewn to be substantially the same as the original one, we can define the extent of the ground towards the south, for the court would of course be made as large as possible. Nothing is recorded to tell us how far the ground extended towards the west, but the sum was a large one, and we may safely assume that the scholars would be able to purchase with it enough land to reach as far as the common pasture.

At the north-east corner of the site, as thus augmented, we find in the 27th Edward I. (1298—9) mention made of "a messuage with buildings, gardens, courts, yards, and other appurtenances," which must have been of some extent, as it had a house 56 feet long by 21 feet broad next the street at its south-east corner. It abutted on the north upon the churchyard, on the south upon the property "of the scholars of the Bishop of Ely," and on the west upon a tenement belonging to the said scholars[3]. This

---

[1] [College Order, May 27.]

[2] "Predictus Episcopus vizt Hugo de Balsham ... in extremis laborans ... scolaribus ad edificia de novo construenda trecentas Marcas legauit de quibus quandam aream ex parte australi dictæ ecclesiæ comparaverunt, et in eadem quandam aulam perpulcram de novo construxerunt; libros etiam plures theologice [sic] et quosdam aliarum scientiarum legauit..." Ex Historia Eliensi, MSS. Harl. 258, fol. 86 b. [Bentham's Ely, ed. 1812, p. 151.]

[3] [College Treasury, "Situs Collegii," B. 9. Sabina, widow of John de Aylsham, conveys to Richard Conyton and Herbert de Shepereth "totum meum mesuagium integrum cum omnibus suis edificiis gardinis curiis curtilagiis ... in parochia Sancti

shews that their site at that time extended from Trumpington Street on the east to a considerable distance westward, and that part of the western piece extended northward as far as the

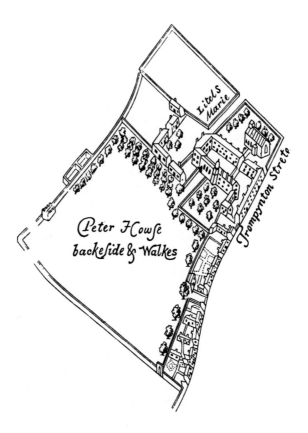

Fig. 3. Peterhouse, reduced from Hammond's Map of Cambridge, 1592.

Petri extra portas de trumpitone inter Cymiterium predicte ecclesie ex una parte et mesuagium Scolarium Domini Episcopi Elyensis ex altera. Et abuttat in uno capite contra regalem viam, et in alio capite contra tenementum predictorum scolarium. Excepta una domo quam perquisivi de hugone le Rede que est situata ex parte australi predicti mesuagii. Et continet predicta domus in longitudine quinquaginta sex pedes, et in latitudine viginti unum pedem." This house she sold to the same persons, 6 May, 28 Edw. I. (1300). Ibid. B. 11. The last deed concerning it is dated 26 Edw. III. (1352—3), when the whole property is sold by Thomas de Wormenhall to three persons. Ibid. C. 4. The dimensions of the house at the S.E. corner being given, (which was evidently only a small portion of the property,) I have

churchyard. I have not been able to discover when this messuage became the property of the College, but certainly not
before 1352—3, the date of its last conveyance.

The first recorded addition to the site after it had reached
these dimensions was in 1307, when the scholars obtained the
manse, or dwelling-place, with the whole of the buildings, be-

Fig. 4. Houses adjoining Peterhouse, from Storer's "Illustrations of the University of Cambridge."

longing to the Brethren of the Penance, or Penitence, of Jesus
Christ, otherwise called "Friars of the Sack[1]." We have now
therefore to inquire into the extent and situation of this.

laid down the frontage of the messuage twice as wide as that of the house: and the
depth as extending along half the S. boundary of the Churchyard. Bp Hugh de
Balsham's hostels would then occupy the site of the Library, and part of the site of
the Chapel.]

[1] [The deed headed " Relaxatio fratrum de pœnitentia facta Collegio de toto manso
eorundem Fratrum," and dated "lennie (Lynn), die dominica proxima ante festum
omnium Sanctorum, A°. D^{ni}. 1307," releases to the College "totum ius nostrum ... in
toto loco nostro cum omnibus suis edificiis in villa Cantebrigie in Parochia Sancti

We learn from one of the Barnwell Registers that the Brethren "purchased the messuage of John le Rus, opposite to the Chapel of S. Edmund, and there got together many excellent scholars and increased in numbers exceedingly[1]." In the letters patent of Henry the Third sanctioning the foundation, the names of the original occupiers of the different pieces of ground bought for the site are given. This deed was issued 25 June, 52 Hen. III. (1268), which fixes the date of the completion of the site[2].

The principal piece was no doubt the stone house (*mesuagium lapideum*) of John le Rus[3], the grounds of which extended from the street to the common pasture. It appears to have been a considerable edifice, large enough to contain the brethren, who erected in one of its courts a Chapel in honour of S. Lucy[4]. North of this was "a messuage with a croft," acquired in 1271 from Walter le Brasur, i.e. Brewer, of Little Shelford, and Audrey his wife[5]. Like the former, it extended from the street to the common pasture. North of this again were two messuages close to the street, acquired from Arnold de Trumpington. One had belonged to Robert Cheshill, a tanner; the other to Robert de Horningsherthe, described as warden (*custos*) of the Chapel of S. Edmund[6]. Behind these was "a selion of arable land," extending to the common pasture like the other pieces. It was sold to John le Rus by William de Madingley, a carpenter, but when the brethren obtained it I have not been able to find out[7]. These houses and land were both bounded on the north by land belonging to the Chapel of S. Edmund, which fell eventually into the hands of the brethren, as it is mentioned in the letters patent above referred to; but when, is not known. The house of

Petri extra Trumpeton gates . . ." Old Register, 59. See also Dugdale, Mon. Angl. vi. 1607 ; and Archæologia, iii. 125.]

[1] Leland, "Collectanea," ed. Hearne, 1. 443.

[2] [College Treasury, "Situs Collegii," A. 11. Appendix N⁰. 1.]

[3] [College Treasury, " Situs Collegii," A. 2.]

[4] [The license for this, dated 1245, ibid. F. 1, speaks of "capellam in curia iohannis rufi grantebrugie extra portam de trumpinton in honore beate lucie erectam." The words of the conveyance are : "ecclesiam in dicto tenemento in honore Jesu X^ti. et sue dilectissime matris."]

[5] [Ibid. A. 12.]

[6] [Ibid. A. 18. The conveyances of Cheshill and Horningsherthe are A. 16 and A. 15.]

[7] [Ibid. A. 1.]

John le Rus had at its south-east angle a small tenement belonging to Stephen Barker[1]; and along the rest of its southern
boundary was the land of Eustace Seled. Barker's house
abutted on the south upon that of Hoel and Thomas Barton[2];
beyond which again lived Stephen the cooper. These several
pieces, probably of no great extent, even when united, indicate a
row of houses next the street, with gardens and pastures behind
them[3].

This is all that can now be ascertained respecting the history
of the site of the Friary. As regards its position, it is stated in
one of the deeds of surrender[4], 2 Edward II. (1308—9), to lie
between the land of Robert de Wynwick on the south, and the
messuage of Richard de Aylsham on the north, and to extend
from the street to the pasture.

There are four deeds relating to Wynwick's property. They
describe a messuage, and an acre of arable land. The former
lies between the cemetery of the brethren on the north, and the
property of Adam Thurston, John Rikeling, and Bernard de
Sawtre on the south, abutting on the street to the east and
on Wynwick's croft to the west. The croft is described as an
acre of arable land in Trumpington Street, between the croft
of the Prior of S. Edmund and the land that formerly belonged
to the Brethren of the Penitence[5]. The Prior's croft is clearly
Volye Crofte, before described, and we therefore know the
southern boundary of this property. Unfortunately we do not
know the extent of the messuages abutting on the street, but

---

[1] [Ibid. A. 7.]

[2] [Ibid. A. 4. Before this could be taken possession of, the brethren were
obliged to obtain permission from the Hospital of S. John. Robert de Huntingdon,
the then Master, gave them leave "ampliare locum suum in parochia sancti petri
quoad duo mesuagia Symonis karettarii et Stephani Bercarii." Ibid. A. 19.]

[3] [One of the conveyances (Ibid. A. 17) gives the dimensions of the house to which
it refers as 22 feet wide, with a "croft behind" it, and the next house as 44 feet wide.
I cannot find out to what house this refers, but it is valuable as indicating the
dimensions we ought to assign to most of these pieces.]

[4] [Ibid. B. 15, 18, 20. It is described as "in suburbio Cantebrigie"..."cum
edificiis desuper existentibus, curiis, vivariis, et aliis pertinenciis."]

[5] [Ibid. B. 12, 13, 19, 25. The acre of land was bought of John Aylsham and
Sabina his wife (B. 19) to whom it had been sold by Eustace Seled (A. 23). This
property has been already mentioned as lying to the south of the western portion of
the Friary.]

assuming them to resemble those near them and to be of small
depth, we can lay down an acre of ground west of them, and
determine the southern boundary of the Friary with tolerable ac-
curacy. We cannot be equally certain about the northern boundary, as we know, from the letters patent of Henry the Third,
that there are some pieces of ground unaccounted for, and the
deeds of Richard de Aylsham's property have been lost.

On the whole, however, we may say that the southern third
of the site within the stone wall before mentioned was occupied
by Wynwick's land, answering to about half the present "Grove"
and two-thirds of the site of the Fitzwilliam Museum. We do
not know when it became the property of Peterhouse. Two
persons of the name of Robert de Wynwick are mentioned in
the deeds, of whom the younger (nephew to the elder) was afterwards Master of the College (1330—38). It is therefore not
improbable that he conveyed the land in question to his College
during this period; but the deed has unfortunately disappeared.

North of this was the Friary, bounded by the street on the
east, by Coe Fen on the west, and extending northwards perhaps
as far as the Hostels and the ground of the scholars. The
history of the ground occupied by the College buildings has
been already discussed.]

CHAPTER II.

HISTORY OF THE BUILDINGS DERIVED FROM THE BURSARS' ROLLS.

[IN the record of the uses to which the legacy of Hugh de
Balsham was put, mention has been made of the construction
of a Hall (*Aula*).] By this word I understand Refectory and
not College, for the latter, as we shall see below, was not
advanced for many years afterwards; and we find the scholars
in 1395 setting forth in their petition to Bishop Fordham for

the appropriation of the church of Hinton that the College was not yet sufficiently endowed, nor their buildings finished, or sufficiently furnished with the offices required, and that the revenues were so very lean and small as not to suffice for the maintenance of a master and fourteen scholars required by the ordinances of his predecessors[1].

The principal materials for tracing the architectural history of the College are a valuable collection of Bursars' rolls of accounts[2], of which the earliest are for 1374—5, 1388—9[3] and 1396—7. For the fifteenth century there remains a broken series of thirty-one, and those for the subsequent centuries are nearly complete. From these we obtain most authentic information concerning the building operations, although, as usual in this class of documents, it is often difficult to ascertain to what part of the edifice the operations of each year belong, and the loss of the rolls of intermediate years necessarily obscures the history. However, the roll of 1374—5 contains an account for the mere ordinary repairs of the House[4], viz. for tiling the Hall and other chambers; for "powntyng" the chambers;

---

[1] Bishop Fordham, in his charter of appropriation of Hinton, dated March 20, 1395—6, rehearses the petition. "quodque dicte nostre domus seu Collegii fructus redditus et prouentus adeo sunt tenues modici et exiles quod ad sustentacionem unius Magistri seu Custodis ac quatuordecim Scolarium qui in dicta domo seu Collegio secundum ordinationes predecessorum nostrorum . . . esse deberent . . . non sufficiunt hiis diebus." [Hinton, commonly called Cherry-Hinton, is 3 miles S.E. of Cambridge. The vicarage was formally appropriated to the College by Simon Langham, Bishop of Ely (1362—1376), but as no appropriation can take effect until a vacancy happens, and as this did not occur in the lifetime of the Bishop, his successors defeated the College by instituting Vicars of their own before the College could assert their rights. Bishop Fordham, however, put the College effectually into possession, and they presented their first vicar on 18 Jan. 1401. The appropriation was confirmed by a Bull of Pope Gregory XII. dated May, 1408. See the Old Register, page 67 seq.]

[2] [The first two of these extend from Michaelmas in one year to Michaelmas in the next: the third from All Saints Day 1396 to Easter 1397. The following rolls have been preserved for the fifteenth century. They all extend from Michaelmas to Michaelmas. 1403—4. 1411—12. 1414—16. 1417—18. 1424—6. 1430—1. 1438—9. 1441—2 (mutilated). 1445—6. 1447—8. 1450? 1455—59. 1460—65. 1466—7. 1469—71. 1472—3. 1474—5. 1488—9. 1491—2. 1493—4. 1499—1500. Total 31.]

[3] [This Roll has been copied, with a translation, by Mr Riley, First Report of Historical MSS. Commission, 79.]

[4] The heading of this part of the account is "In reparacione Domorum, viz. aule, et aliarum camerarum tegulatione ix li. iiij sol. iij d." among which payments we find

and so on, which shews at least that they had a Hall and chambers at this time.

[From the roll for 1403—4, we learn the existence of a "capella," probably a private oratory, annexed to the Master's Chamber[1]. In the next, that for 1411—12, we find the roofing of the kitchen recorded, and the building of a wall called "le Newwall" outside the College, probably on the west side[2]. In the next three, those for 1414—15, 1415—16, 1417—18, repairs only are set down.] There is then an interval until 1424—5, when we find ourselves in the midst of a new building, to which a separate heading is allotted—"Expense nove fabrice in collegio hoc anno." This heading is continued in the roll for the next year 1425—6, and in that for 1430—1; but the items are only payments to masons, slaters and smiths for daywork; for carriage of stone, timber from Thakstead, mantelpieces, windows, and the like, with no indication of the purpose of the edifice, which was probably a range of chambers[3].

In 1431, an indenture occurs between the College and John Wassyngle, of Hinton, a mason whose name occurs repeatedly in these accounts, for building a Library. This indenture, dated Feb. 12, 9 Hen. VI. (1431), is between John Holbrook Master of the College and the fellows of the same on the one part, and John Wassyngle of Hynton of the other part. The said John Wassyngle engages to build in the ground and above the ground the walls, doors, and windows of a

---

"It^m. Sclaters pro powntyng de aula xiij so liiij d. ob." The heading of the Roll is "Compotum Magistri Willelmi Irby incipiendo a festo Sancti Michaelis Anno Domini M°CCC°LXXIIIJ°. usque ad annum revolutum de bonis omnibus domus sancti petri medio tempore receptis."

[1] ["Et in stipendio Carpentarii emendantis tectum Capelle annexe Camere magistri."]

[2] [The mention of wooden poles, "pali," clay and straw shews that it was of mud, supported on a wooden frame. The labourers sometimes slept in College, "Et pro lectis conductis eisdem operariis per diversas noctes per tempus operum predictorum ijs. jd."]

[3] In the roll for 1425—6 a payment of twopence is made to poor scholars (sizars) for carrying wood. "De ijd. solutis pauperibus scolaribus portantibus lignum." [A similar entry in the accounts of Queens' College for 1495—6 is quoted by Mr Searle (History, 127), "Item duobus pauperibus scolaribus laborantibus circa pontem, ijd."] The entire cost of the work was £110. 2s. 3½d. in the first year, and £24. 12s. 7½d. in the second.

certain Library within the aforesaid College, as follows : before
the last day of the succeeding April he shall have ready all
the doors necessary for the said work, and ten windows (count-
ing two small ones as one) of good hard stone from the lower
bed of the quarry of Philip Grove, completely prepared for
setting ; the walls shall be commenced before the same day
of April, and raised to the height of ten feet above the ground
before the next following feast of S. Peter ad Vincula (Aug. 1).
All other windows whatever necessary for the said work shall
be wrought and ready for setting before the second Easter
after the date of these presents (Ap. 20, 1432), and the walls
completely built to the same height as the other walls of the
new buildings of the College before the Feast of S. Michael
the Archangel next following.   He is bound in forty pounds to
the fulfilment of his contract, and the payments he is to receive
are thus enumerated.   For the great door, 5s. 6d.: for every
small door, 3s.: for every large window, 5s.: for every small
window, 2s. 6d., including the shaping and setting: for every
complete week during which he himself shall labour within
the College on this work he is to receive 3s. 4d., and for
every incomplete week at the same rate according to the
number of days: also a gown if he behave well[1].

No dimensions are given, but the specification that the walls
are to be completely built to the same height as the other walls
of the new buildings of the College, shews that the Library
was part of a set of new buildings then in progress.   Its position
is known to have been on the west side of the quadrangle,
where its roof and stone staircase may still be traced.

In the roll for 1438—9, the next that has been preserved,
we find the heading "Expense librarie et noue fabrice." [The
walls had been built in the intervening years, and they were
now making the roof and windows, and laying the floors.]
Carpenters are working at " plancheryng " and " schulderyng
de le gystes," that is, cutting the shoulders of the joists: [and
a number of trees had been felled in the College garden to
provide planks for the floor].   Ten shillings are paid to Reginald

---

[1] [This curious document, copied from the original in the Treasury of Peterhouse,
"Collegium" A. 11, is printed in the Appendix, No. 11.]

Ely the stonemason for making the staircase. The mention of a payment for "bryke" is valuable because the walls of the existing chambers next the Churchyard are partly constructed of brick[1].

[The rolls for the next two years have unfortunately perished, and that for 1441—2 is imperfect. Then there is a break in the series till 1445—6, when a single line suffices for the work done to the Library: a carpenter is employed for fifteen days.] In 1447—8[2] the fittings in woodwork and windows are going on. [Carpenters were sent for from Ely to contract for making the desks: the ironwork for the windows was ordered, and the doorway set. In 1450 the desks of the old Library were broken up, and sixteen locks and two keys were ordered; which marks the period of the transfer of the books from the old to the new apartment[3]. Each lock no doubt required the presence of two officials of the College to open it, as at Trinity Hall and elsewhere.]

In the roll for 1450 the new work of the kitchen, and the making of the upper chamber over the buttery, together with the partition wall between the buttery and pantry, was going on[4].

Then follows a continuous series of rolls from 1455 to 1465 (wanting only 1459—60) in every one of which the heading "Expense nove fabrice" has its place. The work consists of

---

[1] "Et de x[s] solutis Reginaldo Ely lathamo pro factura gradus noue librarie ... Et de xv[s]. viijd. solutis pro mille et ccc[is] et dī [350] tabulis serratis de arboribus succisis in orto collegii. ... Et de xx[s]. solutis pro iii[ml] de Bryke..."

[2] 1447—8. ["Et de viijd. solutis carpentariis venientibus de Ely ad paciscendum pro factura descorum librarie. Et de vli. iijs. iiijd. solutis carpentariis pro fabrica descorum librarie in grosso. ... Et de vij d. in uno lapide pro volta ostii librarie. Et de viijd. solutis lathomo aptanti dictum ostium. Et de xxijd. in xv hamis ferreis pro fenestris orientalibus ... Et de xvij s. x d. in vitriacione duarum fenestrarum librarie et alterius parve fenestre super gradus librarie. Et de viijd. in hamis ferreis pro fenestris occidentalibus librarie. Et de ijs. vd. in quingentis de broddis ferreis pro descis librarie."]

[3] 1450. ["Et de vjd. in resolutione descorum librarie antique. Et de viijs. iiijd. in xvj. seris pro descis librarie et ij[bs]. clavibus."]

[4] "Et de xliij s. iiij d. Willelmo Herward pro factura solarii super promptuarium cum pariete dividente botlariam et pantleriam in grosso." In 1449 Magister T. Lane gave £3 to the work of the new fabric and of the kitchen. Bishop Wren's extracts from the Register of Peterhouse, MSS. Baker, xlii. 197.

masonry for walling, window jambs and monials, iron work, &c. In 1460 the Master's chamber was begun, for the heading "Expense fabrice camere Magistri" occurs for the first time in that year, and the whole sum spent under it is £21. 4s. 2½d.

In 1461, £25. 17s. 3½d. were spent, and in 1462, £28. 5s. 7d., but in these two years there is no specific indication of the nature of the building[1]. In 1463, a carpenter, John Bacon of Halsted, is employed as well as the masons.

Fig. 5. Doorway in ancient boundary wall, from the outside.

In 1464—5, amongst other mason work, mantel-pieces for the parlour and the room over it[2] are mentioned : also windows, timber, tylpyns, "rofetyle," and the placing of them.

In 1466—7, the "Expense nove fabrice" include various cart-loads of clunch sent to the College, together with foundations

[1] [It is called simply "novum opus." The two poor scholars are again employed "ad cariandam terram."]

[2] [" Et de iiij s. in iiij lapidibus pro le mantils caminorum in parleto (parletorio?) et camera superiori." That this was a rebuilding, and not a new work, is proved by the following entry in the roll for 1464—5. "Et de x^d. solut ... pro reparacione antiquorum ferramentorum que erant in fenestris veterum fenestrarum camere magistri."]

of new chambers, and of the "Parleyre" and a room called "the inner chamber[1]."

After this year there remains a broken series of rolls beginning with that for 1469—70 which I have carefully searched as far as 1520, without finding any notice of buildings with the exception of small repairs, so that the College was completed for the time about 1467.

[In 1491—2, the Hall was repaired, and it was tiled on the north side[2], a work which was still going on in 1501—2[3], in which year it was also paved, and in 1502—3 the making of "ly harth" is recorded, which is interesting as shewing that an open fire of some sort was then in use[4]. In 1501—2 a stone wall was erected near the water (*juxta aquam*) at a cost of £23. 12s. 2d. This can be no other than the wall mentioned in Chapter I., to defray part of the expenses of which John Warkworth (Master, 1473—1500) gave one hundred shillings to the College[5]. It is built of large blocks of clunch, with a few blocks of stone added in some places, especially at its northern extremity. It has been a good deal patched with brick, and a coping of red brick has been added along a portion of it, as shewn in fig. 5, which represents an ancient doorway (C, fig. 1), which gave access to the fen, and is evidently part of the original construction. Over this door on the outside are the arms of John Hotham, Bishop of Ely (1316—1337), and on the inside those of John Alcock, Bishop of the same see (1486—1500).]

---

[1] ["Pro opera fundi parleyrie et camere interioris, et pro positione lapidum in fundo omnium camerarum dicti operis," i.e. the "novum opus."]

[2] The following item in the roll for 1469 is curious for the latinization of the technical word "pointing." "Item iij li. ix s. iiij d. solut' cuidam tectori pro reparacione et punctuatione lij. polorum, precium le pole xvj d."

[3] ["Et de x^s. pro posicione tegularum in Aula, et de iij s. iiij d. pro factura ly synk in Aula, et de xvj s. pro pavyng ... in Aula."]

[4] [1502—3. "Et de viij d. pro factura ly harth in aula."]

[5] ["Item dedit 100 solidos monete Anglie ad novum murum lapideum ex parte occidentali collegii." Old Register, 99.]

CHAPTER III.

Comparison of the existing Buildings of the College
with the Accounts. Library, Kitchen, Hall, and
Buttery. Combination Room. Master's Chamber.
North Range. Other Buildings.

THE information conveyed by this valuable series of building
rolls can only be summed up by comparing it with the buildings
themselves, assisted by the annexed map and plan (figs. 1, 2),
assuming for the moment the dates of some of the modern
buildings whose history will be given below.

The present College consists of a principal quadrangle
measuring 86 feet from north to south, by 148 feet from east to
west[1]; and of an entrance court next to the street rather broader
than the quadrangle, and of a mean length of 80 feet, the
north side being much shorter than the south. The chapel,
built in 1628, stands in the midst of it, its gable forming part
of the east side of the great quadrangle, the remaining portions
of which side are made up by two cloisters, originally forming
part of the design of the chapel. The south side of the entrance
court is bounded by the College Library built about 1590, and
the north side by a range of chambers erected in 1738, so that
the whole of this entrance court is now of post-Reformation work.

The great quadrangle appears within to be entirely modern,
but is substantially the mediæval College to which our account
rolls of the fifteenth century belong, as its venerable outer
surfaces in the churchyard on the north, and in the gardens
and kitchen court on the south, abundantly attest. The outer
wall to the west is unfortunately masked by a white brick
facing to bring it into harmony with the modern Gisborne

---

[1] [Like most mediæval courts and structures it is asymmetrical, the south side
being 3 feet longer than the north.]

buildings, with the exception of a small portion at its northern extremity.

We may now compare more particularly the separate parts of the buildings with the accounts. These have shewn us that a Hall and some chambers existed before 1374, and that in 1424 extensive building-works were going on, probably a range of chambers, whose position is not indicated. We then come to the Library, concerning which the rolls have shewn us that the contract for building it was drawn up in 1431, that in 1438—9 the staircase was constructed by Reginald Ely, and that in 1447—8 the carpenters were at work upon the desks.

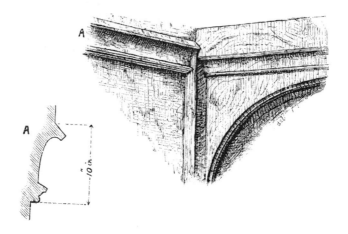

Fig. 6.   Details of roof of Old Library.   A.   Wall-plate and profile of same.

This Library remained in use until it was superseded by the present one at the end of the sixteenth century. It occupied part of the western side of the quadrangle, where it may easily be traced at present by its large staircase and its roof. The incongruous ashlaring and sash windows of Burrough applied to its eastern face in 1754, and the white brick facing with which its western face was equally disguised in 1825, have completely destroyed its ancient exterior, and its interior was divided into chambers after the new Library was built. The staircase, however, of Reginald Ely, a handsome stone vice or spiral staircase, nine feet in diameter, still gives access to its floor (A, fig. 2), and the lower part of a half principal (fig. 6) at the north end of its roof may be seen by ascending the old wooden staircase at the north-west external corner of the quadrangle (B, fig. 2)[1]. [There is a similar principal at the south end, at the head of the stone vice mentioned above.] The rest of the roof is concealed by the ceilings of the chambers into which it is now divided. Enough however remains to shew that the library must have been about forty-five feet[2] long, and twenty feet broad. [Three of the old windows have been preserved; the one at the north end of the apartment, assuming it to have extended as far as the north wall of the College, and the two northernmost in the western wall. The last are plain two-light windows, pointed, without cusps, and set in a square head. The northern one is of three lights.]

The new kitchen comes next in order in 1450. This is at the extreme end of the southern range of building. Its wall (DE, fig. 2), as seen in the kitchen court, is of rough uncoursed rubble work, very different from that of the older buttery and hall, of which it is the continuation. The junction of the two works is marked by a buttress (D, fig. 2) represented in figure 7. The kitchen has a small vestibule divided from it, at the angle of which next to the court is a stone vice (C, fig. 2), which gives access to the chambers above the kitchen and buttery[3]. The chamber over the latter is recorded

Fig. 7. Buttress at junction of Hall and Kitchen.

[1] [This stair and the garrets above are termed in the College "Noah's Ark."]

[2] [I do not understand why Professor Willis assigns so short a length to this room. There appears to be no reason why it should not have extended as far as the north wall : or at any rate up to the southern face of the north range, which would give it a length of 60 feet. The Catalogue in the Old Register, made in 1418, shews that even then the College possessed an extensive collection of books, which had probably grown too large for the *libraria antiqua* mentioned above (p. 12, *note*), and this new room was built to accommodate them.]

[3] [The original doorway at the foot of this stair was discovered and opened out

to have been reconstructed at the same time with the kitchen ;
when also the buttery was divided by a wall which still remains.

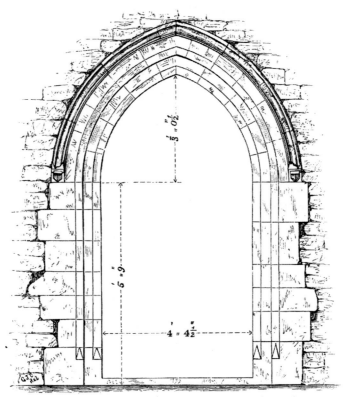

Elevation of Hall Door: (South)

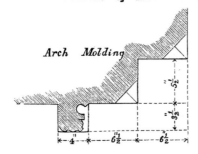

Arch Molding

Fig. 8.   Door at South End of Hall-passage.

in the course of the work done to the south side of the court in 1870. The present
Treasury is on the first floor at the head of this stair : and a door from it opens
into the gallery of the Hall.]

The south wall of the hall is now curiously patched with successive repairs, but was originally carefully built of small squared clunch, much more neatly jointed than any of the other clunch walls in the College. A plain pointed doorway at the south end of the passage behind the hall screen (F, fig. 2) is the oldest piece of masonry remaining in the College buildings. It has sometimes been called Early English, and at any rate appears to be earlier than 1307. [It is represented, with its moldings, in figure 8, and a ground-plan of that at the opposite end of the passage, which is much richer, in figure 9; a third door, still richer, gives access to the Hall from the vestibule at I (fig. 2).]

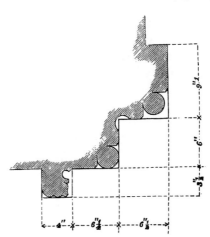

There are no traces of buttresses to the hall, and the present windows have been patched into the wall in such a manner as to make it impossible to trace accurately the original state of it. The eastern extremity is of rougher work as if rebuilt, and the parapet of the whole is all of subsequent work. The squared clunch work extends to the buttress in the kitchen yard and in

Fig. 9.   Ground-plan of door at North End of Hall-passage.

cludes the buttery, thus marking a first portion of the work, namely the hall as first erected. There can be little doubt that it is substantially the same as that erected with the Bishop's legacy shortly after 1286. [The only notices of it that occur in the Bursars' Rolls are for repairs and fittings. Wooden door-jambs and doors were made in 1563—4; and in 1589—90 it was wainscotted, apparently for the first time, as much as £12. 10s. being spent upon the work. It had previously been hung with tapestry, probably over the dais, which was repaired in this year[1].]

---

[1] [Bursar's Roll, 1589—90, "xxiijs. vjd. Gilberto Thorn reficienti le Cloth of Arras in aula."]

From the east end of the hall a series of chambers in two stories extends to the present library. The first floor is known to have been the Master's lodge. The ancient statutes of 1344 give the Master two chambers, of course placed in the ancient buildings nearer the street, but the later statutes which belong to the beginning of the sixteenth century assign to the Master "all the eastern portion of the house which adjoins the hall, except the common chamber, which we desire to be open to the scholars in winter[1]."

This common chamber or College parlour has also been time out of mind placed on the ground floor at the east end of the hall, and the mantels of its chimney-piece appear to be mentioned in 1464. But on the other hand the foundation of a parlour in connexion with other chambers occurs in 1466, after which date there is a break in the rolls, and the position of these chambers cannot be fixed. [The parlour is frequently alluded to in the rolls, usually for repairs only. In 1550—1 the fireplace was painted in colours, and in 1589—90 the floor was paved with tiles[2].]

At the junction of the hall and Master's upper room a tower staircase is placed (G, fig. 2), as at Pembroke, S. John's, Christ's, and Queens', by which he could descend to the garden and to the hall and combination room[3]. The patched state of the wall in this part is partly due to a fire which consumed the Master's chambers in 1639, and occasioned a repair of them and of the tower which is recorded in the rolls[4]. [The woodcut

---

[1] [Commiss. Docⁱˢ. ii. pp. 6—56. The seventh Statute, *De assignatione camerarum*, ordains "Magister ... unam cameram pro se eligat quam voluerit, et aliam de consilio Decanorum." In the later code, Statute 35, the words are "Magister eam totam (excepto communi Conclavi, quod Scholaribus tempore hyemali patere volumus) Domus partem sibi habeat, quæ ab orientali parte ejusdem Aulæ est contigua."]

[2] ["Et de lij⁵. Homes pro sexcentis le pauing tyle pro conclaui."]

[3] [On one of Professor Willis' papers I find the following description of this part which seems worth preserving, "Examining the south wall from the east end of the Hall, we first observe an external brick turret with a vice, and then a piece of brick walling much patched and altered by the insertion of sash windows and repairs. This extends as far as the beginning of the Library." These windows, with the curious wooden louvre which at that time capped the turret, are well shewn in a view by Westall, Ackermann i. 2. See below, Chap. VIII.]

[4] 1638. "Edificationem novorum graduum a conclavi superiori in hortum magistri descendentium."

1639. Materials, etc. "ad restauranda cubicula et hortum præfecti 7 li. 12 s. o d. ...

(fig. 10) shews the present appearance of this tower. The battlements were added, it is believed, during a general repair of the College in 1848, but no record has been preserved of the manner in which it was terminated originally. The door giving access to the garden is original. Over that which opens into the Master's chamber on the first floor is a molding which seems to indicate a roof. Possibly the staircase was originally of wood, and rose no higher than this door.]

Fig. 10. Tower-staircase.

The order of description has now led us from the old Library on the west side of the quadrangle, to the Master's lodge and chambers at the end of the south range. But as the previous rolls from 1424 to 1429 relate to chambers, and the indenture for the Library in 1431 alludes to these new buildings of the College, we can only suppose part of the north range to be

pro turriculæ fabrica et materie, etc. ... pro fabrica collegii et cubiculi præfecti igne consumpti, cum horto Præfecti" etc.—total, 132 li. 7 s.

1640. "... pro materia et opera plumbaria circa turriculam ij li. xiiij s. j d."—
Bursars' Rolls.

The previous existence of the tower is proved by Lyne's plan in 1574: else it might have been imagined, from these items, that it was built in 1638.

meant, which consists wholly of chambers and may now be described.

It must be previously remarked that the outer wall of the north end of the western range is built of roughly squared clunch in courses, not of the same period as the neatly finished work of the hall, and totally different from the uncoursed rubble of the kitchen. At this corner is a pointed doorway, originally belonging to a thoroughfare passage into the quadrangle (B, fig. 2). This was blocked up when the walls received their Italian dress, and a new passage was cut through the centre of the west side to reduce the court to classical symmetry. This new passage at its other end now enters the modern Gisborne court with mediæval asymmetry at one of its corners.

On the north side of the principal court, opposite to the Hall door, there was originally a second thoroughfare passage leading into the churchyard (H, fig. 2), of which the two parallel walls still remain on the ground floor within a set of chambers; and the archway of the north side, now bricked up, is to be seen in the churchyard. The inner arch, with a sundial over it, which opened into the quadrangle, is shewn in Loggan's view, but is now masked by an Italian window, the fourth in order from the N.W. corner. A stone vice like those on the other sides of the quadrangle leads to the upper chambers at the east end of the north range (P, fig. 2).

It will be remembered that the parish Church was used as a College Chapel until after the Reformation, as was the practice at Corpus Christi College; and, as at that College, the north side of this quadrangle is connected with the Church by a gallery leading from the upper floor, and bridging over the space between the vestry and the College[1]. From this gallery a flight of stone steps leads down to the choir door. The space under this bridge, as the remains of the walls shew, was once vaulted over, and had open arches on the east and west sides for the parishioners' road into the churchyard, which had been on the south side of the Church, as the porch was, until 1737, when the new building next the street was planned. A College order was made on March 3 of that year:

---

[1] [A ground plan of the parts of the Church and College here described, on a scale of 16 feet to 1 inch, is given in figure 18.]

"That the new Building to be erected be set from the chapel as far as the vestry, and a church-way be made for the parishioners on the north side of the church; provided the consent of the Parish and Ordinary be obtained for that purpose."

The vaulted passage had also a gateway arch on the south side leading into the College (A, fig. 18), of which the western jamb (ibid. B) still remains, and a door on the north side into the vestry (ibid. H).   The new building obtrudes itself into the area of this passage, and the vault and two of the arches were pulled

Fig. 11.   Western face of Gallery and Vestry.   From a photograph.

down to make way for it.   The gallery is now carried upon a wooden floor, and only the western wall and arch remain, with a few traces to bear testimony to its ancient form[1].

This wall next the churchyard shews that the vestry and archway were planned when the Church was built in 1350, for

---

[1] The passage from the College to the Church was not destroyed in 1737, for an order in 1750 (May 9) directs "that a Porter's lodge be fitted up in the passage from the Cloyster to Little S. Maries' Church."

the lower story of the vestry is in continuity with the walls of the Church, and like that has its plinth of hard stone with clunch masonry above. [This is well seen along the west wall CD, and the wall of the Church, DE.] The north jamb of the archway (ibid. F) is carried up as part of the same structure to a height of four or five feet; but the south jamb of the archway, the arch itself, and the walls of the gallery and upper story of the vestry are a totally subsequent work, added apparently after a considerable interval, and wholly built of red brick. [A view of the gallery, and adjoining structures, is given in fig. 11; it is also indicated in Hammond's plan (fig. 3).] The north wall of the chambers against which the gallery abuts is part of the same brick structure, extending forty-eight feet to the west; at which point (L, fig. 2), at the end of a set of chambers, an abrupt change of work occurs, and the remainder of the wall to the corner (ibid. R) is of clunch. The clunch on this side is very much decayed, and the whole wall presents a mass of patchwork, alterations, and inserted chimneys and windows. [One of the original windows is here shewn (fig. 12). Those that were inserted subsequently, except the obviously modern ones, are shallow square-headed double lights.] The lower part of the wall is of brick for a few feet above the ground, which may however be a facing added to the decayed clunch by way of under-pinning it[1].

The most probable time for the completion of the gallery appears to be the middle of the fifteenth century, when the choir of the Church was refitted, altars consecrated, and chantries founded; and this was also the period when the new quadrangle was in building, according to the rolls already quoted.

The rough construction of the building, the unfortunately perishable clunch which was so largely employed, and the desire for larger windows, led to several thorough repairs, by which the original architectural appearance of the College was destroyed, long before it assumed its Italian disguise.

---

[1] [It should be noticed that the wall of the Church at the foot of the stairs (G, fig. 18) is very much corroded, as though by exposure to weather. This, coupled with the fact noticed by Prof. Willis above, that the lower part of the wall CD is of clunch, while the upper part is of brick, makes me think that the gallery was built long subsequent to the staircase. It had been planned before, but the design had been abandoned for some now unknown reason.]

[The following notices of extensive repairs during the first half of the sixteenth century occur in the rolls.

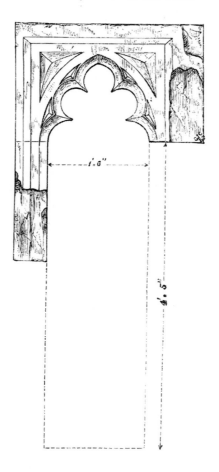

Fig. 12.   Early Window in North Wall.

In 1523—4 Thomas White was paid twenty-two shillings "pro ly poyntyng" of eleven "rods" of the Library[1]. In 1526—7 John Morley "pointed the whole northern side of the house next to the Church" at a cost of twenty shillings: and in 1538—9 workmen were employed for twenty-two days upon the same

---

[1] [A "rod" is 272¼ square feet in Cambridgeshire.]

part, and upon the Library, Hall, Master's chamber, walls of the grove, and other places in the College. This cost £3. 8s. 3d. In 1544 a quantity of plate, apparently belonging to the Chapel, was sold to pay for a new pavement to the court[1]. In 1545—6 the west side of the College was repaired over an extent of seven stadia and two ells; also the south side of the kitchen and the chamber of Mr Cycell over an extent of three stadia and a half: and the outside of the College on the north over an extent of thirteen stadia. The whole sum spent in repairs this year was £7. 10s. 11½d.[2]

The existence of the following buildings in or near the College is proved by the references to them in the accounts; but, unfortunately, in most instances it is impossible to fix their position. They are interesting, however, as illustrating the domestic requirements of an ancient College.

A bakehouse (*pistrinum*) is mentioned in most of the rolls of the fifteenth century; also a place to keep salt provisions in (*domus salsamentorum*[3]): "le fish loft[4]," intended probably for salt fish; and "le fish house in le Coe Fen[5]," probably a vivarium. There was a storehouse for coal (*domus qua carbones exponuntur*[6]), and a lime-house (*domus qua calx ponitur*)[7]. Besides these there were a granary (*granarium*)[8], a "haye house[8]," a "wheate loft[9]," a dove-cote[10], and a hen-house[11] (*domus gallinaria*). We know from Loggan where the tennis-court (*sphæristerium*) was. I have not, however, been able to discover when it was built. It is first mentioned in the roll for 1571—2, after which time the name occurs very frequently down to 1605—6, the last year in which

---

[1] "Rad. Aynsworth, M.A. M^r. et Socii, omnes ac singuli 12, vendiderunt crucem et calicem argentea deaurata, et alia Jocalia, ut pavimentum plateæ conficere possent, 1544." Register of Bishop Wren, MSS. Baker, xlij. 188. There is an amusing entry in 1547—8, "vj d. pro reparatione muri in promptuario a furibus perfossi."

[2] In 1545 the Commissioners of Henry VIII report that three fellowships had been vacant for several months by reason of the great expenses in repairs during the last year. Commiss. Doc^{ts}. i. 112.

[3] Roll for 1559—60.   [4] Ibid. 1591—2.
[5] Ibid. 1587—8.   [6] This took three years to build (1568—71).
[7] Ibid. 1564—5.   [8] Ibid. 1588—9.
[9] Ibid. 1587—8.
[10] [Ibid. 1545—6. It was let on lease in 1675, and again in 1682, at a yearly rent of 20s.]
[11] Ibid. 1545—6.

any allusion is made to it[1].   There was also a treasury (*domus thesaurorum*), and a chapter-house (*domus capitularis*)[2].

A building is described at some length in the roll for 1544—5, the very name of which it is difficult to understand.   It is called "spectaculum or New-work."   It was built of freestone, was of some height, as it required a scaffold, and was paved[3].   It was repaired in 1589—90 and other years, but the use to which it was put is never so much as alluded to.   There is a small building with battlemented walls shewn upon Hammond's map (fig. 2) abutting on the west wall of the College, and overlooking the fen. If the conjecture that this is the "spectaculum" be accepted, it would then signify "look-out."   In confirmation of this view it may be mentioned that in Loggan's print of Queens' College, reproduced in the History of that College, a similar structure is shewn, built over a doorway[4] in the garden-wall next to the river, and of such a height that the floor is level with the top of the wall.   It has battlements, and is approached by a flight of broad external stairs.]

[1] [It was let on lease in 1667, and again in 1677 at a yearly rent of 12*d.*, the College reserving the use of it for the Fellows free of charge, and, "Provided also that the Scholars...shall freely play with their owne Balls and Rackets from eleven of ye clock untill one, paying nothing for the same; and at other times when ye Mr or Deans...shall allow them."]

[2] Ibid. 1589—90.   "Et de xiv d. Greene pro iron barres et staples pro domo capitulari, et de xxij d. pro sera et claue pro eadem ut patet in billa præfecti."

[3] "Et de ijs. vjd. persone aurige pro vehendis decem bigatis lapidum vocat' ly fre ad reficiendum murum spectaculi vocati ly newwarke.·... Et de v d. pro funiculis ad colligandum ly scafowolde apud ly newarke.   Et de iijs. Magistro Sherwood pro bigata lapidum ly fre pavyngestone pro ly newarke.   Et de vjs. viijd. Magistro collegii pro duobus bigatis et dimidio eiusdem generis lapidum ad sternendum ly newarke."

[4] [This was the position of the structure at Peterhouse, from a payment made 1590—91 "ix d. Greene reficienti seram ostii sub le Newarke."]

CHAPTER IV.

BUILDINGS OF THE SIXTEENTH AND SEVENTEENTH CEN-
TURIES. DR PERNE'S LIBRARY. WORKS OF DR MATTHEW
WREN.

IN addition to the old chambers and buildings of the great
quadrangle, there were others extending to the street, whose
position can only be understood by following the history of the
present buildings of the entrance court, the earliest of which is
the Library on the south side, due to Dr Andrew Perne (Master
1553—1589), as appears from the following singular passage in
his last will[1] :—

"The Colledge Librairie of Peterhouse...I doe wishe to be newe
builded at the east end of the Masters Lodginge longewayes towards
the Streate by some good Benefactor or Benefactors that I have spoken
toe and wiche have promised to helpe to the buildinge of the same.
That is Mr Customer Smithe, Mr Machell of Hackney, and Mr Thomas
Sutton of Newyngton principallie, and if noe other man will contribute
to the buildinge of the sayed Librairie w^{t}in one yeare after my dis-
cease, then I will soe muche of my plate to be solde and other of my
goodes and moveables, as will build the same three score foote in
length and the breadth and heighthe to be as the rest of the Colledge
is, w^t loftes and chimnies; and all the foresayed newe librarie to be
newe builded as is aforesaide, w^{t}in three or foure yeares at the furthest
after my dicease.   I will all my bookes bequeathed in this my testament
to be layed and chayned in the old Librarie of the Colledge and the
foresayed Masters or Presidents[2] to preserve all the Bookes that I have

---

[1] It was signed 25 Feb. 1588, and probate taken May, 1589. [The following
extract is taken from a copy in the Diocesan Registry at Peterborough. I have not
been able to discover the original. His private library had become famous, for when
the French Ambassador visited Cambridge on Aug. 30, 1571, " he went to Peter Howse
to see Dr Pearne's Studdie or Librarie, supposed to be the worthiest in all England."
MSS. Baker, xxiv. 250, Cooper's Annals, ii. 278.]

[2] [The Masters of Peterhouse, S. John's and Queens', or the Presidents thereof,
had been mentioned in a previous clause of the will.]

given in this my will to the sayed Librarie as appeareth afterwardes, the which I will to be written in three severall Register Bookes indented, the on to remayene in the Custodie of the M[r] of Peterhouse for the time beinge and his Successors, the second in the Colledge comen Chistes, the third in the handes of the keeper of ye Colledge Librarie of Peterhouse, the w[ch] keeper I will to be bound w[t] twoe Suerties in three hundreth pounds for the safe keepinge of all the sayed bookes and the makinge goode of them at the saied accompt in the said librarie yearelie to bee made before the Vice chauncellor the Master of the said Colledge of Peterhouse and the Master of S[t] Johns or in their absence before their Presidents, after the drinkinge in the Parlor the which shall be imediatlie after the sermon is ended[1]; and that the sayed keeper suffer none of the sayed bookes to be lent to anie person out of the sayed Librairie; but he to see all my bookes that I shall give to the Librarie to be bound w[t] chaines at my coaste And the names of the bookes that be sett in euerie stall to be written in the end thereof, w[t] my name in euerie of y[e] said Bookes; and that the senior Bursar be bounde at ye takinge of his office for the makinge at that time before the said persons a trewe accompte of all other thinges that I doe give to the Colledge....And I will that the sayed[2] Scholler and keeper of the said Librarie shall have a chamber under the said Librarie, and he to be in the sayed Librarie dayely two houres at the least, except it be holie daye or except he have licence of the Master of the Colledge being called thither and to goe thither when he shall be required by anie of the Fellowes of Peterhouse aforesayed...."

[Accordingly in the Bursar's Roll for 1590—1 material in wood and stone is bought; and the work must have proceeded rapidly at first, for in the following year the door leading to the Library from the Master's chamber was made, shewing that the ground floor must have been complete or nearly so. During the next year no work is recorded: but in 1593—4 the greatest activity prevailed. The floor was laid, casements were fitted to the windows and glazed, hinges and bolts to the doors, the walls were plastered and the beams coloured. The work must have been finished in this year, for not only do we find a charge for making the "half-pace" or raised stage on which the bookcases were to stand, but "platts" for the shelves are bought; and lastly the books were moved in, for one Crofts was employed to take

---

[1] [He had previously directed that this sermon is "to be made for me yearlie in the parish Church of litel S[t] Maries on the Sundaye in the afternoone next ensueinge that daye in the which it shall please God to take mee out of this presente life to his mercie."]

[2] [It had been previously directed that the Librarian should be a scholar, and receive 5 marks annually.]

the chains off (probably from those in the old Library), and ten shillings were distributed among the scholars for writing the catalogue[1].

In this same year (1593—4) the room over the Library, called in the accounts "le gallery," was built, with windows in its north and south walls, and a triple window at the end (towards the street). Access to this was originally obtained only by the turret stair (G, fig. 2); for that by which it is now approached from the landing close to the Library door at the head of the stair leading up from the cloister (M, fig. 2) is modern, and was doubtless made when it was divided into chambers. This gallery was assigned to the Master before it was built, as the following order shews, which was probably made at the time of the completion of the basement.

"Oct. 25, 1591. It is ordered by me which in the vacancy of the Bishopric of Ely am your Colledge visitor that the whole upper Roome over D[r] Pernes new Library and halfe of the Roome under the said Library in Peterhouse shall be part of the M[rs] Lodging.

JO. CANTUAR.[2] "

The entire work was not completed until 1594—5, when a quantity of oak board, and casements, both double and single, were bought, at an expense of £50. 8s. 1¾d.]

The Library was built as directed at the east end of the Master's lodging, stretching from that towards the street, but its south wall next to the garden shews that it consists of two portions built at successive periods. The first part next to the old lodge is exactly sixty feet long, as Dr Perne's will directs (NO, fig. 2), and this is constructed of rubble interspersed with large stones. The point of junction with the Lodge (N) can be easily seen, the rubble of the south wall of the Lodge being composed of much smaller stones. The second part, which elongates it by thirty-six feet, so as to reach the street, is of brick, and has a brick gable with an oriel window in the street bearing the date 1633, above, in brickwork.

[1] [The account for this year under the head " Fundatio Doctoris Pearne " is transcribed entire in the appendix, No. III. It is an excellent specimen of the Bursars' Rolls of Peterhouse, shewing the curious mixture of Latin, French and English in the language, and the method of setting down each expense in the order in which it was incurred, without any attempt at classification.]

[2] Old Register, 86.

[We now come to a period of great activity in improving and increasing the College buildings, due mainly to the architectural taste of Dr Matthew Wren, of whom we read in the Parentalia:

"In 1625 he was rather call'd than preferr'd to the Mastership of St Peters College in Cambridge; where he exercis'd such Prudence and Moderation in his Government that he reduced all the Fellows to one sacred Bond of Unity and Concord, and excited the Scholars to Constancy and Diligence in their Studies. Moreover, he built great Part of the College from the Ground, rescued their Writings and ancient Records from Dust and Worms, and by indefatigable Industry digested them into a good Method and Order.

But seeing the publick Offices of Religion less decently perform'd, and the Service of God depending upon the Courtesy of others, for want of a convenient Oratory within the Walls of the College; what then he could not do at his own Charge, he compass'd by his Interest in well dispos'd Persons abroad, and procur'd such considerable Sums of Money, that he built and beautified a complete Chapel, which he dedicated March 17, 1632[1]."]

Passing over for the present the building of the Chapel (1628—1632) which shall be told at length in a separate chapter, we come to the first change made in the court after the building of the western portion of the present Library in 1590. This work was undertaken in consequence of unexpected legacies bequeathed to the College, as is set forth in a College order, dated April 9, 1632, of which the substance is as follows[2]:

"Whereas Dr John Richardson, formerly Master of this College [1609—15], and afterwards of Trinity College [1615—25], has bequeathed £100 to build a brick wall next the street to the east, and other benefactors enumerated have left money for founding four Scholarships; we, the master and fellows of Peterhouse, after due deliberation, decree: that the ancient and ruinous range of chambers extending from Dr Derham's chamber to the gate of the churchyard, and from the latter to a point opposite the Library, be forthwith pulled down, provided however that the materials, as far as possible, be used up again, and fitted to the new building: and that from Dr Derham's chamber a range of chambers in three stories be built for the reception of fellows and students like those in the other parts of the College, and that from these to a point opposite the Library there shall be

---

[1] [Parentalia: or Memoirs of the Family of the Wrens, fol. London 1750, p. 9. Dr Wren's Catalogue of the College Documents is still in use.]

[2] [The original is a verbose composition in Latin.]

constructed a brick wall with a large and handsome door in the middle[1]."

Lyne's plan of Cambridge (1574), and that of Hammond (1592), were taken before Perne's Library was built; the former shews a range of buildings next the street, and a few houses between them and the street; but the latter, which is the more precise, shews a wall at the east end of the court running from the end of the Master's lodge northwards to the opposite range, and separating off a narrow court next to the street (fig. 2). This court has buildings on the north and east sides, and extends slightly more to the south than the principal quadrangle. No entrance is shewn from the street, and it is probable that up to this time the College had its principal entrance from the churchyard, through the vaulted porch under the gallery. It is evident that the eastern range stood clear of the site of the Chapel, which was completed by March 17, 1632, while the order for pulling down the chambers is dated April 9, 1632. Dr Derham's chamber was at the east end of the north range[2], and we have seen that the churchyard street-gate was at that time at the south-east corner of the churchyard (fig. 1). We learn therefore that old chambers occupied the north and east sides of the entrance-court, and extended beyond Perne's Library. Some of these chambers were probably older than those of which we have followed the building from the account rolls, and are those which were repaired in 1374. Part of them may also have been included in the works of the fourteenth century.

The new chambers which were built in consequence of the order of 1632 on the north side of this court are shewn in Loggan's view (fig. 14), which also represents two doors into the street instead of one. This must have been the result of a change

---

[1] The holders of the above-mentioned four scholarships are to be paid their stipends out of the rents of the new chambers. On Oct. 21, 1663, it was ordered that the six chambers lately constructed or fitted up on the border of the churchyard be appropriated in future to the Fellows of Mr Park's and Mr Ramsay's foundation. This must apply to the north range ordered to be built in 1632, and shews how College work lingers.

[2] The Chapel Account-book shews that in 1629, when the Chapel was begun, they took down "the wall between the Master's lodging and Dr Derham his chamber," to clear the ground. Therefore the Doctor's chamber was opposite to the Master's on the other side of the court.

of plan during the execution of the work, for the style of their or-
nament corresponds to the date. By the date, 1633, on the brick
gable of the Library we see that its elongation to the street
followed immediately upon the demolition of the old chambers.
The date probably belongs to the beginning of the work rather
than to the completion, for it was not till 1641—2, that a
payment of £30 to joiners (*scriniarii*) for making three new
cases for the Library shews that the additional space was being
fitted up[1].

The Bursar's Roll for 1637—8 shews a total expenditure of
more than £200 upon a "Restauratio extraordinaria" of the
College, which includes £97 for workmanship upon the decayed
and corroded windows and outer doors in both courts, besides
stone, brick and other materials for the same[2]. To procure
additional funds for these works a letter soliciting subscriptions
had been issued in 1636, in which the Master and Fellows
state that they have built a Chapel which still remains insuf-
ficiently ornamented, and unfinished, that they have rebuilt

---

[1] Mich^s. 1641 to Mich^s. 1642.

"Pro purganda Bibliotheca post fabros scriniarios	0 . 11 . 11	
Pro libris emptis	11 .	
Pro fabris cæmentariis et latomis	7 . 4	
Pro fabris scriniariis pro extruendis tribus novis thecis	30 . 0 . 0 "	

[Some new fittings however had been put in previously; for in 1633—4 we find
"xiij li Ashley pro novis sedilibus in Bibliothecâ." The work done in 1641—2 was
clearly the beginning of the fitting up, for in the following year 1642—3 three more
cases were made at the same price; and in 1643—4 apparently two, at a cost of £19.
In 1644—5, £11 . 5 . 0 is paid "pro theca nova et tabula;" and in 1645—6, £12 . 0 . 0
for the same, together with £10 . 0 . 0 "pro fenestra orientali." In 1647—8, £11 . 17 . 0
is paid "pro thecis novis et tabulis;" and in 1655—6 the vestibule is fitted up, as
appears by the following:

"Scriniario pro fabrica novi vestibuli et scriniorum	17 . 6 . 8	
Carpentario pro opera circa fabricam novi vestibuli	0 . 9 . 6	
Fabro ferrario pro ferramentis circa novum vestibulum et scrinia	3 . 5 . 10 "	

The "tabula" may perhaps be the frame to contain the catalogues, though the word
usually meant a shelf in the 17th century. These bookcases will be figured and described in the chapter on College Libraries.]

[2] "Pro lapide cæso, Lateribus coctis, Calce viva, Arena, Lignis, etc. ad Re-
staurationem extraordinariam Collegii in ædificandis, removendis, atque in ordinem
redigendis omnibus fenestris infra aream ejusdem Collegii tam novam quam anti-
quam ... et exterioribus ostiis tabe et carie prius consumptis."

and repaired the ruinous chambers, and are now endeavouring to increase the Library, and put in order the Hall and the Court[1].

In 1638—9, ten pounds was paid to John Westley, for repairing and restoring the roof of the west side of the College[2]. Thus the court was brought to the aspect it presents in Loggan's print.

CHAPTER V.

WORKS OF THE EIGHTEENTH CENTURY.

[THE idea of completing the College by a second court towards the east had been entertained by Dr Perne, in whose will the following clause occurs :

"Item I doe give towardes the buildinge of the east ende of the Colledge of Peterhouse aforesaid like to the rest of the Colledge havinge a fayer gate house in the midst of it like to St Johns gate house twentie powndes to the said Colledge of Peterhouse ; to be payed out of my goodes by mine Executor within three yeares after my decease, to be reserved in the Colledge chest to that purpose only. I trust that the Master and Fellowes of Peterhouse for the time beinge will be earnest and dayly sutors for the buildinge of the same goodlie worke with the helpe of my Lord of Caunterburies grace that nowe is Archbishop Whitgifte, Mr Customer Smythe, Mr Sutton of Ashton, Sir Wuliston Dixie, and Sir Thomas Ramsie, all wch have promised to contribute towardes the buildinge of the same . . . ."

Whether the complete realisation of this plan, so as to include an east front, was ever seriously considered we do not know. Nothing however was done in this part of the College after the civil war, until] Dr Richardson's range of chambers on the north side of the entrance court was doomed to destruction on March 30, 1732, when it was

"Agreed . . . yt ye Building on ye North side of ye Chappel be taken down wth all convenient speed and rebuilt in a decent and strong manner wth ye College dead-stock[3]."

---

[1] [The letter is printed in the Appendix, No. IV.]

[2] "Pro reparando et restaurando tecto Collegii a parte occidentali Johanni Westley, xli."

[3] College Order, March 30, 1732.

This resolution however was not carried out for several years afterwards. Mr Burrough of Caius College prepared a design, for which he received a piece of plate of the value of ten pounds "in consideration of the Trouble he has been at on the College Account[1]:" and four years afterwards a copper-plate engraving was ordered "representing in Perspective the Chapel, with the New Building now erecting on the Northside, and another design'd to be erected on the South[2]." Engravings of proposed buildings were usually made at this period and circulated to assist in obtaining subscriptions. The south building, however, was never carried out. The north building is a handsome and substantial Italian pile of chambers in three stories, of brick, faced with Ketton stone on the south and east sides[3].

[It was directed to be commenced at the end of the year 1736, by the following order :

"July 21, 1736, Agreed . . . that the Order made in the year 1732 to take down the Building on the North Side of the Chapel be put in Execution at or before Mich[s]. next, And that an Estimate be taken of

---

[1] College Order, Feb. 6, 1735—6.

[2] [College Order, Aug[t]. 11, 1739. This plate, drawn by R. West, and engraved by P. Fourdrinier, shews a building on the south exactly similar to that on the north; and between each of them and the Chapel a building of the same height and design, supported on a cloister of three arches in rustic work, like the arch that now gives access to the northern building.]

[3] [Outside the easternmost window of the second floor on the north side are two iron bars on brackets, with a third attached to them, just far enough from the wall to allow a man's body to pass. Tradition assigns this window to the rooms of the poet Gray, who had these bars put up to secure his escape in case of fire by means of a rope. One night some malicious wags shouted "Fire!" The poet descended; not, however, on to the ground, but into a tub of water placed under his window. This is said to have been the real cause of his leaving Peterhouse for Pembroke. A month before he left he writes to Dr Wharton : "I beg you to bespeak me a rope-ladder (for my neighbours every day make a great progress in drunkenness, which gives me cause to look about me). It must be full 36 feet long, or a little more, but as light and manageable as may be, easy to unroll, and not likely to entangle. I never saw one, but I suppose it must have strong hooks, or something equivalent at top, to throw over an iron bar, to be fixed in the side of my window." In the first letter from Pembroke to the same, March 25, 1756, he evades his real reason for removal : "I left my lodgings because the rooms were noisy and the people of the house uncivil." He had been disturbed, says Mason, by "two or three young men of Fortune." Their names are given by Moultrie in his edition of Mitford's Life of Gray. Dr Law, Master of Peterhouse, called the affair "a boyish frolic" and refused redress. See Gray's Works by Mason, Moultrie, and in the Aldine Edition, 1853.]

the Incomes, in order to allow them to the several Persons to whom they belong :"

but the next order, made in April, 1738, shews that the work had been again deferred, and that the old range of chambers was still standing ; also, that some other material than stone had at first been decided on ; for it was then

"Agreed that the new Building be cas'd with Stone towards the Chapel and the Street, and that the Stone for this purpose be provided immediately ; and that the Building be taken down as far as the Cloyster."

The question of position had been considered from the first, for on April 6, 1734, it was agreed :

"That in consideration of the Parish's giving their consent for the taking in seventy-five feet in length and nineteen feet in breadth of the Churchyard for the erecting a new building, the College do pay to the said Parish an Acknowledgment of five shillings per annum, and make a pav'd walk on the North side of the Church ten feet in breadth, together with a large Door five feet in breadth, and a small Door into the Chancel with Porches for each Door. And like-wise that a new Gate be made to the Churchyard, the trees on the North side cut down, and the large Pew by the North Door removed."]

By this means additional breadth was given both to the entrance court and to the chambers. [The delay above mentioned was very likely due to some hesitation on the part of the Parish, for it was not until March 23rd, 1737—8, that it was

"Agreed that the new Building to be erected be set from the Chapel as far as the Vestry, and a Church-way be made for the Parishioners on the north side of the Church, provided the consent of the Parish and Ordinary be obtain'd for that Purpose."

The work was sufficiently advanced by the beginning of 1741[1] for an agreement to be made "that the Ceilings in the new Buildings be performed, viz., to be floated and finished in the best and workmanlike manner, including whitening at 1 shilling and 3d. per yard :"—and in June of the same year the rooms were painted[2]. They were not ready for occupation apparently until the beginning of 1742, when their rents were

---

[1] May 5, 1741.
[2] College Order, June 12, 1741.

settled by a College Order[1]:] and in the following year it was agreed :

"That the Bursar give Mr Burrough fifty Pounds in Consideration of his Designing and overseeing the Execution of the new Building[2]."

He was at this time therefore acting as a professional architect.

Finally, on Nov. 13, 1744, it was

"Agreed . . . that the Bursar be empowered to place a Fence of Rails, and put Bars into the Lower Windows of the new Building towards the Church Yard and likewise to pave the Area before the said Building."

In 1751[3] the new gates toward the street which are still employed were erected in lieu of those which were set up in 1632. [Up to 1848 the College was bounded on this side by a high brick wall with a stone coping nearly as high as the architraves of the stone gateways, except for the short interval between the north gate and Burrough's building, where a low wall and iron railing, such as now extends along the whole street front, seems to have existed from the beginning (fig. 4)[4]. In 1848 considerable repairs were executed, in the course of which the present wall and railing was set up, and the gateways enriched with a half pilaster set against their sides[5].]

In 1754 it was determined to modernize the great quadrangle, which had now, in consequence of the gradual rebuilding of the entrance court, acquired the name of the Old Court. I subjoin a series of successive and contradictory resolutions all passed in this year, which afford an amusing illustration of the manner in which Burrough, now Sir James, and Master of Caius College, persuaded the College to change the stucco and small sash-

---

[1] [April 30, 1742. There had evidently been some unusual difficulty in getting the work completed, for on July 26, 1740, it was agreed "that the workmen employed about the new Building be paid no more money by the Bursar on Acc^t till they bring in a measurement of the whole."]

[2] College Order, March 15, 1743—4.

[3] [College Order, April 15, 1751.]

[4] [This is shewn in the plate at the head of the University Almanack for 1813: in Storer's Illustrations and in Le Keux, i. 233.]

[5] [College Order, May 20, 1848, "for new roofing, repairing, and improving parts of the College."]

windows at first projected, for the full Italian dress which was finally imposed upon the old walls [1].

March 4, 1754. "At a Meeting of the Master and Fellows it was agreed that the old Court be new stuccoed: that the two walks be laid with new freestone and the remainder be paved with pebbles, that the window and door Cases be repaired, and the grass plats new laid. This work to be immediately undertaken and conducted at the direction of the Master, Deans, and Bursar, who shall likewise determine what alterations shall be made in the Sheep court.

May 2, 1754. Agreed...to make new sash windows in the old court.

May 23, 1754. At a meeting of the Locum tenens and Fellows it was agreed that instead of stuccoing the old court according to an order of the Master and Fellows bearing date March 4th, 1754, it be cas'd with Ketton Stone, the Front of the North side to be finish'd this year. The window and doorcases instead of being repair'd to be fitted up with stone of the same kind. That instead of the sashes meant in the order dated May 2^d, 1754, modern sashes be put in, and as this may occasion some expense in the fitting up that part of the inside of the rooms adjoining to the windows the charge which may from hence arise shall be borne by the College. This work to be conducted at the direction of the Master, Deans, and Bursar and the price of stone and workmanship to be settled by the Master of Caius College.

Sep. 17, 1754. At a meeting of the Locum tenens and Fellows it was agreed that instead of the Battlements a Parapet Wall be erected, adorned with a Dentil Cornice, and that the old materials be made use of as far as they will go. Agreed also that the Price of the Workmanship employed in the Cornice shall be three shillings p^r foot according to the Proposal made by Mr Elsden.

Dec. 19, 1754. Agreed...that the West and South Sides of the College Court be cas'd with Stone in the same Manner and on the same Directions as mention'd in the order dated May 23, 1754.

Jan. 6, 1755. Agreed ... y^t an Arch be made thro' ye middle of ye west end of ye Court and y^t Mr Markland and Mr Pemberton have satisfaction made for any Damage to their chambers occasion'd by ye alteration above.

June 28, 1755. Agreed ... that the order of March 4, 1754, relating to the Area of the Court be cancelled and that there be made in it only one large grass plat without any walks of freestone.

Feb. 26, 1756. Agreed that the Money formerly paid for Musick at Christmas be applied to the supplying the Lamp att the new Building, and four new Lamps which are to be placed at the four corners of the new Grass Plot [2]."

---

[1] [For more details respecting this architect, see the History of the Schools and Senate-House. He was elected Master of Caius College, Feb. 27, 1754.]

[2] [The two on the east side are shewn in Ackermann's view of the court. They are lofty stone obelisks. The present iron lamp-posts were put up in 1830. College Order, Dec. 22, 1830.]

[In 1774 the west side of the College was new roofed, at an expense of £300; and in 1783 a sum of £400 bequeathed by the Bishop of Waterford was ordered to be applied to a similar work on the north and south sides[1].]

In 1791, the wall of the chambers and library on the south side of the entrance court was plastered, which, to judge from the condition of the wall of the same building next to the garden, was the only thing to be done for the sake of neatness short of ashlaring or rebuilding. Thus the ancient College was brought to its present aspect. [The rooms under the Library were converted into a Porter's Lodge, a Lecture Room, etc., in 1821[2].]

Two wings containing chambers were built to the west of the quadrangle by the munificence of the Rev. Francis Gisborne, a former fellow, in 1825[3]. The first stone of these was laid on the 30th of August in that year. [The south wing was first built, and the northern decided on a few months later. The whole was completed at the end of 1826[4].] These wings extend ninety feet westward, and are at the same distance apart, so as to form, in conjunction with the west wall of the old College chambers, a square court to which the founder's name has been attached. They are erected in the modern Gothic style, of white brick, from a design by William M'Intosh Brooks, Architect, who designed the castellated Town Gaol on Parker's Piece[5]. [The builder was Mr Thomas Tomson of Cambridge.]

---

[1] [College Orders, April 3, 1773, March 26, 1774, April 19, 1783.]

[2] [College Order, March 30, 1821.]

[3] He presented £20,000 to the College in 1817.

[4] [College Orders, May 30 and October 21, 1825, June 16, 1826, and Feb. 12, 1827. The last payment to the contractor was made on May 12, 1828.]

[5] [This was erected soon after June 23, 1827, on which day the royal assent was given to an Act for Building a new Gaol for the Town. Cooper's Annals, iv. 554.]

CHAPTER VI.

HISTORY OF THE CHAPEL.

THE construction of the existing Chapel in lieu of the parochial chancel was begun in 1628 : for although an Oratory [1] is
mentioned in previous records, yet the positive assertion of the
act of consecration of the Chapel on March 17, 1632, that " from
the first foundation of the College to the present time it had
no sacellum within its walls," is sufficient to shew that that was
not a regular Chapel, but only a licensed room for private
devotions; and did not supersede the performance of the greater
services in the parish Church [2].

[1] On Oct. 12, 1388, John de Fordham, Bishop of Ely, gave license, to last for
his own good pleasure, to the Master and fellows and all persons residing with them
to hear divine service in a chapel within the said house, and to perform other divine
offices therein. Fordham's Register, MSS. Baker, xxxi. 208. [See also above, p. 10.]

[2] [The words of the Master's speech to the Bishop at the time of Consecration
are as follows ... "cum intra muros Collegii Sacellum non habuerint, coacti sunt
extra portas Collegii in vicinum Templum exire quotidie; idque tempore brumali
horis antelucanis et postlucanis, quod in non raram opportunitatem maleferiatis
Tenebrionibus cessit ulterius evagandi. Porro cum idem Templum ad oppidanos
quoque jure parochiali pertineret, neque horae canonicae Petrensibus vacabant
Sacrae Eucharistiae in Festis Principalibus aliisque Dominicis celebrandae neque
quotidiana sacra iis ritibus atque apparatu obire poterant quos ex SS. Matris Ecclesiae Canone puriorisque Seculi exemplo observare par erat, praeter alia quoque
incommoda, quae versiculis aliquot fusius comprehensa ... schedulae huic annec-
tentur..." Old Register, p. 480, copied, MSS. Baker, v. 245. To this Baker appends
the following note. "The verses spoken of in the beginning of this service are
Crashaw's *Votiva Domus Petrensis pro Domo Dei*, printed then in a single sheet,
and after among his Poems. And begin thus *Ut magis in mundi votis*." A short
quotation from this now forgotten work may be interesting. After comparing the
rising hopes of the members of Peterhouse to the dawn of day, he exclaims,

" Quando

Quando erit, ut tremulae flos heu tener ille diei,
Qui velut ex oriente novo jam altaria circum
Lambit, et ambiguo nobis procul annuit astro
Plenis se pandat foliis, et lampade totâ
Laetus ut e medio cum sol micat aureus axe,
Attonitam penetrare domum bene possit adulto

This Chapel, 64 feet long, by 26 feet broad, was erected in the Mastership of Dr Matthew Wren [Master 1625—34]. It was set in an isolated position, halfway between the Library on the south, and the range of chambers on the north. It is connected at its west end to the buildings on either side by a gallery with an open arcade below offering a very picturesque and characteristic specimen of the architecture of that period[1].

The clearing of the ground for the foundations was begun in May 1628, by taking down the "litle Ostle," and "the wall betweene the M^rs lodgeing, and Dr Derham his chamb^r[2]." The foundation was laid on June 30, 1628. George Thompson was the freemason, but there is no record of the person who made the design. The work seems to have gone on continuously, but slowly, [no work being done in the winter, from November to April, during which months the walls were covered up[3].] The masonry of the windows was paid for in Nov. 1629, and they were glazed in 1632[4]. The roof dates from April 1629, to September 1631. [The floor was paved with glazed tiles from Ely. The seats and altar furniture were provided in 1632, in which year the consecration took place,

> Sidere, nec dubio pia moenia mulceat ore?
> Quando erit ut convexa suo quoque pulchra sereno
> Florescant, roseoque tremant laquearia risu
> Quae nimium informis tanquam sibi conscia frontis
> Perpetuis jam se lustrant lachrymantia guttis?
> Quando erit ut claris meliori luce fenestris
> Plurima per vitreos vivat pia pagina vultus?
> Quando erit ut sacrum nobis celebrantibus hymnum
> Organicos facili et nunquam fallente susurro
> Nobile murmur agat nervos; pulmonis iniqui
> Fistula nec monitus faciat male fida sinistros?"

Complete Works of Richard Crashaw, ed. A. B. Grosart, 2 vols, 1873.]

[1] [Professor Willis calls it in a note a "curious specimen of Jacobean Gothic."]

[2] [The small size of "the little ostle" may be inferred from the facts that the whole cost of pulling down was only £1. 14s. 10d.; and that no more than 3 men were ever employed upon the job at one time.]

[3] [Chapel Accounts. "About ye couering of the walls when the workemen left of the first winter after it was begun." "Item for uncouering the walls in Aprill next after 0 . 5 . 0."]

[4] [These windows, as soon as set up, were protected by wirework, as appears from "The wyerworkers Bill" preserved among a number of small accounts discharged by Dr Cosin. The whole cost including "tenters, spikes, nayles and wyer to fasten it" was £15. 17s. 10d.]

at eight o'clock in the morning of March 17th. Thus the whole work occupied nearly four years[1].]

It appears from the Bursars' accounts that the subscriptions amounted to £2365, including £300 from Leonard Mawe, Master (1617—1625), and Bishop of Bath and Wells[2], and £300 from Dr Cosin, afterwards Master.

From the following document, which is not dated, but which must have been drawn up soon after the consecration, we gather that the Chapel was erected on the sensible plan of fitting it for use as rapidly as possible, leaving such decorations as were not absolutely required to be provided by subsequent benefactors, or as funds accumulated. Thus the side walls and the east end were constructed of rough brickwork[3]; and the desiderata for the interior are enumerated, as a marble "frontis-piece" for the Altar, a silk pallium, the painted glass of seven windows, the ornamental case of the organ, and the historical paintings of part of the walls.

"Sacellum Collegii Sancti Petri in Academia Cantabrigiensi a fundamentis nuper exstructum et consecratum Mar. 17, A.D. 1632.

		£
Expense.	Prima et nuda structura	1000
	Chori subsellia	130
	Vasa et Ornatus Altaris Locique circum-jacentis	260
	Pavimentum Marmore polito stratum	180
	Ornatus Fornicis	186
	——— Fenestrarum sacris Historiis depic-tarum	118
	——— parietum Fenestris interpositarum...	180

[1] A Bursar's account book is preserved, which was exclusively kept for the building of the Chapel, and to it I am indebted for the particulars above given. Everything is minutely recorded even to "June 7, 1628. pack thread to measure out the ground for the wall, 13d.;" and "June 21. ... to Pattison in regard of spoiling his boots in standing in the water to dig. 0.0.6."

[2] [This was a bequest "pro tecto plumbeo."]

[3] [The building accounts of the Chapel include charges for clunch and bricks, but not for stone, except "for water-table 284 foote and for coines 156 foot"—"for 10 windowes at 8ₗᵢ. a peece"—"for 598 foote of splayes"—"for corben table over yᵉ 9 windowes." "Item for 290 foote of freestone Quines for yᵉ butterys at 10ᵈ. yᵉ foote——£12.1.8." These entries shew that the brickwork was supplemented by a certain amount of stonework. The four sides of the Chapel, together with the cloisters, before the east side of their northern division was lengthened to meet the building of 1742, measure exactly 284 feet.]

	£
Vestimenta et stragula Phrygia	50
Sacristia, Capsulæ, et Organile	60
Organum pneumaticum.........................	140
Libri chorales......................................	40
Porticus et nova Facies Sacelli de sectis lapidibus	140

Summa   2484

Expense (pro quibus Collegium nunc in Ære alieno) superant summam receptam £119.

Et desunt adhuc
> Frontispicium Altaris de marmore polito
> Pallium cum frontalibus holosericis
> Septem Fenestræ sacris Historiis depingendæ
> Ornatus Organi pneumatici
> Structura lapidea ad orientalem sacelli faciem quæ nunc Lateritia est et invenusta
> Utrumque Sacelli Latus similiter restaurandum cum Acroteriis.
> Ornatus interiorum Parietum nondum depictorum Historiis."

The exterior facings of the Chapel were entirely built at the expense of Dr Cosin, who succeeded Bishop Wren as Master of the College in 1635. He was ejected at the rebellion in 1644, and restored to the Mastership in 1660, but being immediately made Bishop of Durham, was succeeded in the former office by Dr Hale. The pavement was due to the munificence of his wife, Mrs Frances Cosin[1]. His affection for his College did not however cease when he left Cambridge, for the Order Book records (2 Feb: 1665)

"Sixty pounds being now received wch my L^d of Duresme sent to ye College as one Moitie of the Sum wch his L^p was pleased to promise for ye building of ye East end of our Chapel with freestone ; the said £60 were this day layd up in ye Chest in ye Treasury, sealed in a Purse. . . . The Mony is to ly there till it be taken out to pay ye Workmen."

His will, dated Dec. 11, 1671, contains this clause :

" I give and bequeath two hundred pounds towards the reedifying of the north and south sides of St Peter's Colledge Chappell in Cambridge, with hewn stone-worke answerable to the east and west ends of the sayd Chappell allready by mee sett up and finished[2]."

---

[1] [Benefactors' List, Blomefield, 156.]

[2] [A previous passage in the will records the donation of £120 for the east end of the Chapel: and a memorandum, bearing the same date, states that the

The west end and its porch[1], which had been built before the summary printed above was drawn up, are carefully represented in Loggan's print (fig. 14), and a comparison of that with the existing building shews that its general appearance has suffered very little from the meddling of modern restoration.

Fig. 14. West front of the Chapel and North Cloister. From Loggan.

£200 had been paid "for the faceing the south and north sides thereof with hewen stone and new canted buttresses." The will is printed in the Correspondence of John Cosin, D.D. Ed. Surtees Soc^y. 1872, ii. 291.]

[1] [This porch had been the object of special donations.

"Rev' Pat' Matthaeus Wren D' Ep' Norw', ex piis Donationibus ad Structuram Porticus assignavit £30. Petrus de Laune, S. T. P. ex hoc Coll' £25. Joh' Cosin S. T. P. Magr' Coll' £10. Socii £11." Benefactors' List, in Blomefield, 155.]

The porch was taken down in 1755, and "the materials applied to yᵉ Repair of yᵉ Court." The foliation has been cut out of the window, and the carving of foliage, etc., in the frieze and in the spandrils of the lower arcade has been scraped off. Lastly, the tabernacle which occupied the space above the window has been exchanged for a clock. The whole composition belongs to the beginning of the reign of Charles the First,

Fig. 15. North Cloister, as rebuilt in 1709.

but the east end, erected after the Restoration, is in a plainer style, and is capped by a small pediment[1].

[Dr. Cosin, who shared Archbishop Laud's views about Church ceremonial, introduced a gorgeous ritual into this Chapel, together with the use of incense. In consequence, it attracted much ill-will from the Puritans. One of his most bitter opponents says :

[1] [A careful drawing of the east window will be found in the Cambridge Port-folio, ii. 488.]

"that in Peter House Chappel there was a glorious new Altar set up, and mounted on steps, to which the Master, Fellowes, Schollers bowed, and were enjoyned to bow by Doctor Cosens the Master, who set it up; that there were Basons, Candlestickes, Tapers standing on it, and a great Crucifix hanging over it. . . . that there was likewise a carved Crosse at the end of every seat, and on the Altar a Pot, which they usually called the incense pot : . . . and none of them might turne their backs towards the Altar going in nor out of the Chappell : . . . and the common report both among the Schollers of that House and others, was, that none might approach to the Altar in Peter-house but in Sandalls, and that there was a speciall consecrated Knife there kept upon the Altar, to cut the sacramental bread that was to be consecrated [1]."]

In the diary which William Dowsing, the iconoclast, kept of his proceedings we read :

"We went to Peterhouse, 1643, Decemb : 21, with Officers and Souldiers and...we pulled down 2 mighty great Angells with wings, and divers other Angells, & the 4 Evangelists, & Peter, with his Keies, over the Chappell Dore—& about a hundred Chirubims and Angells, and divers superstitious Letters in gold ; & at the upper end of the Chancell, these words were written, as followeth *Hic locus est Domus Dei, nil aliud, et Porta Cæli*. Witnes Will : Dowsing. Geo : Long. These wordes were written at Keies Coll : and not at Peterhouse, but about the walls was written in Latine, *we prays the ever*, & on some of the Images was written, *Sanctus, Sanctus, Sanctus*. on other, *Gloria Dei, et Gloria Patri*, etc : & all *non nobis Domine &c* : & six Angells in the windowes. Witnesses Will : Dowsing, George Longe [2]."

Many of these Angels and Cherubim were probably at-

---

[1] [Prynne, Canterbury's Doom, fol. Lond. 1646, p. 73. The account is probably much exaggerated ; but that incense was really used is proved by the list of plate furnished by the Bishop, where a charge is made "for the Sencor :" and for "making a newe case to the Sencor." "Correspondence," etc., i. 224 ; and the Chapel Accounts for 1632—3 record payments for much costly plate, altar-cloths, cushions, and hangings. See Appendix, No. v. Similar accusations are brought against Dr Wren, in two curious and extremely scurrilous Pamphlets, "The Wren's Nest Defil'd," 1640, and "Wren's Anatomy ; Printed in the yeare, That *Wren* ceased to domineere, 1641." The latter expressly accuses him of introducing Latin service into Peterhouse, and setting up an altar there : an accusation the truth of which is proved by an entry in the above account for eight service-books in Latin.]

[2] MSS. Baker, xxxviii. 455. [Dowsing's Diary is printed rather differently in Carter's History of the University of Cambridge, 8°. London, 1753. So far as I have been able to discover, this was the first time that the diary was printed ; but unfortunately Mr Carter tells us nothing about the history of the MS.]

tached to the roof, which is now in very good order, and a characteristic specimen[1].

The stalls and organ gallery appear to be those which were fitted up at the first [though a College Order of April 10, 1666 complains that "our College-chapell is not yet provided of an Organ, nor of more money than £25 towards yᵉ Purchase of one." It was decided soon after that £35 should be spent in buying one. It was expected to have been ready by Michaelmas in that year, but "by reason of yᵉ Plague in yᵉ Town" was somewhat delayed, and I have not been able to discover when it arrived[2], but it was probably in working order in 1669—70][3].

These fittings contain a mixture of genuine mediæval panelling, which was possibly brought from the parochial chancel, or the disused chantries. This may be seen at the back of the stalls, and in front of the organ gallery. The stalls and subsellia, however, belong in style to the period of their construction. The stalls have no misereres. The entrance door of the Chapel is also a mediæval door removed from elsewhere, perhaps to replace that which was defaced by Dowsing. [It has been ornamented with Jacobean shields and enrichments.]

In the interior, the east end was of course utterly defiled and demolished by Dowsing, and the altar had no rails when Blomefield wrote, for he tells us that

"The East Window containing the History of Christ's Passion is very fine and whole, being hid in the late troublesome Times, in the very

---

[1] [We find in the Chapel Accounts for 1631:
"Imprimis for 8 Angells and woode to make the winges of the Angells 43ˢ."]

[2] [College Orders, April 28 and October 25, 1666. In contradiction to these pleas of poverty the following special subscriptions to the organ are recorded in Blomefield, 154:
"Joh. et Dᵃ. Alicia Peyton rogatu Magistri dederunt organum Pneumaticum, quod valebat £40.
Ad instaurandum Organum Pneumaticum Pentecost Hoper (cum filium haberet) ex hoc Coll' Soc'. £20."]

[3] [There had apparently been some legal difficulty about obtaining the organ, for the accounts of 1661—2 record "Expensa circa litem pro organo, £19.8.8." In 1665—6 we find "Pro expensis in tempore pestis £43.3.6." In 1666—7 "Pro organo-poeo ex donatione per Magistrum Ashburnham £20. Organum inflanti 10ˢ." In 1667—8 "Expensae circa organum £44.0.0." 1669—70. "Organum inflanti £2.0.0." This charge is continued yearly from this time, and probably marks the period when the organ was ready for daily use.]

Boxes which now stand round the Altar instead of Rails; the Chapel is paved with black and white Marble, beautified with Sentences, is stalled round, hath an Organ, and two large Brass Branches."

Moreover, that Doctor Beaumont (Master 1663—69)

"drew with Chalk and Charcoal, those two Pieces by the Altar, that on the North side of the Wisemens Offering, being exceeding fine : the Star is admirable[1]."

In 1731—2 about £70 was paid to joiners ("*scriniarii*") for work in the Chapel, perhaps the panelling at the east end. Also in 1735[2] the roof was ordered " to be examined in order to have it taken down or repaired :" but the latter alternative was evidently adopted, and nearly £300 was spent upon the Chapel, of which £105 was paid to the painter.

[The view of the interior of the Chapel drawn by Pugin for Ackermann's work shews large tablets, apparently of stone, on each side of the east window, and between the windows on the north and south sides. They extended from the cornice of the stalls to the corbels of the roof. The Creed and some texts were painted on them. They were removed in the course of a thorough repair of the Chapel carried out in 1821—2[3].]

The present altar is railed round, and has a handsome modern altar-piece of wainscot behind it, but at what period constructed does not appear.

Six of the lateral windows were, between the years 1855 and 1858[4], enriched with painted glass by Professor Ainmüller of

---

[1] Collectanea, 157. [Uffenbach, who visited this College Aug. 7, 1710, says: "On either side of the altar hung two scenes of the Passion, well designed in black on blue cloth in golden frames." Translation by Rev. J. E. B. Mayor, 170.]

[2] College Order, March 27.

[3] [Ibid., Augt. 7, 1821. " Agreed that the Joiners' work in the Chapel, and the Screen in front of the organ gallery be repaired." June 29, 1822. " Agreed that the ornaments and wainscotting in the interior of the Chapel be cleaned and repaired......" July 6, 1822. "Agreed that all the Tablets in the Chapel shall be taken down, and that the Lead Work on the south side of the Roof and the Wainscotting of the cieling be substantially repaired."]

[4] [The offer " to supply the two windows adjoining the East End of the College Chapel with stained glass" was accepted Nov. 28, 1851. These are criticised as "a new and important decoration" in The Ecclesiologist for August, 1855; and the last four in the same journal for April, 1858.]

Munich, the total cost of which, including the carriage and
setting up, has amounted to £1467[1]. Each window contains
about 67 feet 6 inches superficial in glass. [The work was
undertaken as a memorial to William Smyth, M.A., Professor of
Modern History (1807—49), chiefly through the exertions of
the Rev. William Nind, M.A., Fellow.]   The subjects are,

> North side.   The Sacrifice of Isaac.
>   The Preaching of S. John the Baptist.
>   The Nativity.
> South side.   The Resurrection.
>   The Healing of a cripple by SS. Peter and John.
>   S. Paul before Agrippa and Festus.

The south gallery was at first a passage from the Master's
Lodge to the Chapel, and led to the Master's pew in the organ
gallery, which still exists.   It was built in 1633[2], and the north
gallery probably soon after.   They both apparently became
ruinous about 1709, for on April 15 of that year the following
College order was made :

"Y^t ye Cloyster on ye North side of ye Chapel should be taken
down to ye ground and rebuilt according to a Pap^r deliver'd into
ye Society at a meeting y^s day by M^r grumbold . . . : also . . . that
forty five pounds, the price of ye Trees cutt down behind ye new
Gardens be given towards this work."

Two years afterwards the south cloister was taken down
and rebuilt in the same style, as the following order shews :

October 4, 1711. "Agreed . . . . that the Cloyster on the south
side of the Chappell should be taken down to the ground and rebuilt
of the same dimensions it is at present and according to the Model
of ye Cloyster now erected on the north side thereof.   And that y^e
sum of eighty pounds in the Treasury of the Gift of ye Bp. of Durham
be applied towards the Charge of ye said Building. . . ."

These new galleries are in the Italian style, and totally

---

[1] [There were a few fragments of old glass in these windows before the Munich
glass was put in, consisting of heads and portions of figures with arabesques and other
ornaments, drawn in a style similar to that of the east window, and probably at the
same period.   We have seen that Bishop Cosin proposed to fill the north and south
windows with painted glass, and these fragments may perhaps indicate that his design
was carried out, but that the windows were not so fortunate as to escape destruction
in the same way as the east window did.   The fragments have been carefully preserved.]

[2] ["May 4, 1633.   About ye gallery from ye chapell to the lodging, £21 . 15 . 10."]

different from those which they superseded, which were precisely
like the arcade that still remains against the lower part of the
west front of the Chapel, with four-centered arcades and a single
Jacobean Gothic window in the centre of each above. [The
differences between the two are shewn in figures 14, 15. The
former is an exact reproduction of part of Loggan's print. It was
ordered that the south gallery should be fitted up as a chamber
on April 2, 1757.]

CHAPTER VII.

HISTORY OF THE OLD CHAPEL; OR, CHURCH OF S. MARY THE LESS.

[WE must now examine the history of the Church which had
so long been used as the Chapel of the College.]

The episcopal founder appropriated to the use of his scholars
the church of S. Peter outside Trumpington Gates, which accordingly was employed by them as a college chapel until the
beginning of the seventeenth century; and the parish duties
were performed by a parochial chaplain appointed by the
College[1]. The Church fell to the ground about 1350, as Fuller
states, without mentioning his authority[2].

The Registers of the Bishops of Ely furnish the following
dates:

"1340. 17. Kal. Nov. (Oct. 16). License is granted to Nicolas
de Wisebech to celebrate Divine service within the College until the
Church of S. Peter is dedicated.

1349. License for the dedication of the Church of S. Peter outside
Trumpington gate[3].

1352. 7. Kal. April: (Mar. 26). License to the Scholars of the

---

[1] In the list of Patrons of Churches, etc. in the Diocese of Ely, inserted in Bishop
Gray's Register and others, we find "Ecclesia Sancte Marie extra Trumpiton Gates
Cant: appropriata Magistro et Scolaribus Domus S^{d} Petri regitur per Capellanum."
This list is undated, but as it states that the Rectory of S. Botolph is in the gift
of Corpus Christi College it must have been drawn up between 1353 and 1460.
]Cole says "about 1340 or 1350."] MSS. Baker, xxx. MSS. Cole, xxiii. 197.

[2] Fuller, 76. [It had been given to the Hospital of S. John by Henry son of
Sigar of Cambridge, in the reign of King John. Peterhouse Treasury, "Ecclesia
Cantabrigie," A. 1. Selden, Hist. of Tithes, 386.]

[3] MSS. Cole, xxxv. 118.

House of S. Peter to celebrate on a portable Altar in the chancel of
S. Peter's Church, on account of the work of the new chancel[1].

1352. Nov. 3. The Church outside Trumpington gate was dedicated in honour of the Blessed Virgin Mary[2]."

The actual Church is a lofty body without aisles or any
structural division between nave and chancel. It is 27 feet wide
and 100 feet long, divided into six severies, each of which except the westernmost is a double square in plan. It is lighted
by lofty windows, and has deep buttresses. The tracery of the
windows on the north side has wholly disappeared except from
the one at the east end[3]. On the south side and at the eastern
gable are rich flowing Decorated windows, the tracery of which
is designed in the same style, and in many respects with the
same patterns, as those of the Lady Chapel at Ely, and of the
Presbytery of the Cathedral, the former of which was begun in
1321 and finished about 1349, and the latter finished before
1336[4]. The division between nave and chancel is marked by the

---

[1] MSS. Cole, xxiii. 130. "On the back of an original Bull, which Serves as a
Sort of Binding to this Volume [The Registers of Bishops Montacute and L'Isle] is the
following Entry or two, wrote in the same Hand with the Register, but a Peice is torn
off at the Corner, so that the Sence is imperfect." The entries are records of licenses
which the Bishop granted in 1352 for celebration in particular places, of which the
one referring to Peterhouse is: "Item 7 Kal. Apr: ibidem [at Downham] 1352,
similem licenciam Scolaribus suis Domus Sancti Petri super Altare portabile in Can-
cello Ecclesie Sancti Petri predicti pro eo quod inceptum et finitum novi Cancelli...."

[2] " Die Sabbati proximo post festum omnium Sanctorum [Dominus Episcopus]
dedicavit Ecclesiam extra Trumpeton Gates Cantebrig' in Honorem beate Marie
semper Virginis." Register of Bishop L'Isle, MSS. Cole, xxiii. 105. [On Nov. 28
in this year the Bishop gave to the College service-books and "quasdam tabulas
depictas ad ornatum summi altaris;" and in 1357 vestments, altar furniture, and
plate. Register of Peterhouse, p. 82.]

In 1385, Bishop Arundell, at the petition of the parishioners, changed the dedication feast from the morrow of the Commemoration of All Souls (Nov. 3) to the 11th of
July, on account of the number of feast days immediately preceding the old dedication
day, which prevented the parishioners from rendering due honour thereto. MSS.
Baker, xl. 233. [The Bishop's statute is printed in The Ecclesiologist, xv. (1857), 286.

[3] [Professor Willis wrote this description just before the extensive repairs executed
under the direction of Mr G. G. Scott in 1857 : and it is therefore extremely valuable
as shewing what the state of the Church was before they were undertaken. Dis-
coveries were made during the work which render a few alterations necessary. I have
also added an account of the changes in arrangement introduced at that time.]

[4] [Hence, probably, the tradition that Alan de Walsingham (Prior of Ely 1341—
1364), who is known to have designed the Lady Chapel and other buildings there, was
also the architect of this church. It is worth remarking that a vaulted passage

base of the ancient screen (now cut down to the level of the pews), which cuts off three severies to the east for the Chancel [1].

On examining the buttresses on the outside it will be found that those which terminate the first two severies reckoning from the east (*a*, *b*, *c*, fig. 2), have their original plinth and moldings running uninterruptedly round each buttress, and along the wall until we come to the fourth buttress (*d*), along the east side of which they are continued but are not returned along the face. This buttress is in fact patched along the face into a resemblance to the others, but exhibits unmistakeable traces of the former existence of an enclosing wall, and of a roof. The same indications may be observed on both sides of the Church.

[The plinth reappears on the western face of the fifth buttress (*e*), and is continued along the sixth (*f*), which is a plain square buttress with Decorated stages applied to its face [2]. This is the same on the south side. The sixth severy is wider than the others; and the seventh buttress (*g*) is somewhat different; but seems to have been intended originally to resemble the sixth.]

At the north-west corner of the Church, in the west wall, is a fragment of Norman walling consisting of the piers of an arch (S, fig. 2). This is evidently part of the old church of S. Peter, and once belonged to a tower which appears to have been still in existence when Fuller's plan was made in 1635. The whole of the west gable is a piece of modern work. The walling of the last severy, on both sides of the Church, is of a different character from that of the five eastern severies. On the south side it contains a lofty window of Perpendicular tracery, though the bases of the mullions and the sill are Decorated. The foundations of the original porch (ibid. T) remain. In the fourth severy there are indications, on both the north and south sides, which shew that two chantry chapels were constructed opposite to each other by enclosing the space between the buttresses. The construction of

originally led from the Lady Chapel at Ely to the Presbytery, as from this church to the College. (Architectural History of Ely Cathedral: by Rev. D. J. Stewart, plate 3.)]

[1] [This screen was removed in 1857.]

[2] [It was discovered in 1857 that this additional strength was designed to resist the thrust of an arch, the remains of which existed inside the Church (> > fig. 2). It is clear from this that it was originally intended to terminate the chancel here, but that the plan was altered, and the western part finished with later work.]

both of these is the same, and as follows. A low wide arch was formed under the window, beneath which a monument was placed upon the line of the foundation of the wall; and on the west side of this arch a small doorway was constructed to give access to the Chapel. The two arches completely fill the space. The arches on both sides have lately been laid open. Those over the monuments were ornamented with deep moldings and rich complex foliation. The monuments no longer exist. [The wall above the Chapel on the north side was originally pierced by a window of four lights, similar to those on the south side. This was subsequently bricked up on the outside, and plastered over on the inside, so that until the restoration of 1857 the tracery alone was visible. Some fragments of the ancient glass and leadwork were then discovered, and carefully preserved. At the same time the four windows on the north side, then blank, were filled with tracery imitated from those on the south side. The wall above the Chapel on the south side is now blank, but the outline of the window that was once there may easily be detected by the interruptions of the string-course and the joints of the stonework. On the outside the present horizontal string-course, though apparently entire, may be seen to be made up of the curved pieces of the original drip-molding. The door and window into the north chantry, with the window above, are shewn in figure 16.]

At the east end of the Church a vestry in two stories is erected against the south wall of the easternmost severy, and close to this against the next severy there is a second apartment or vestibule, entered by a door from the south side of the choir (figs. 17, 18). This apartment has also a door on the east side into the vestry up four steps, and a third on the south side into the once vaulted space under the gallery (fig. 18, H), thus opening directly opposite to the ancient entrance of the College. Besides these doors it contains an ancient stone staircase which leads to a fourth door above the last, opening to the gallery. By this door and stairs the chaplain and other members of the College were enabled to enter the choir at all times, without passing through the external gate of the College.

The vestry has a piscina, and square windows of two lights each, one on the side next to the College, and two on the

Fig. 16.   Chantry with window over it.   North side of Church of S. Mary the Less.

Fig. 17. South wall of Chancel of S. Mary the Less. A, Piscina. B, C, D Sedilia.
E, Door leading to Vestry.

eastern side. The former retains its cusps and original condition, but the whole eastern face of the vestry is bedaubed with Roman cement, and the details are wholly obscured. The vestry, [but not the room over it,] was contemplated when the Church was built: for the window in the south wall of the easternmost severy against which it is placed is a genuine orb window[1], of rich flowing tracery, panelled with stone in lieu of glass up to 17 feet from the ground (fig. 17). [The upper portion was found to have been glazed when examined in 1857, as the smaller window over

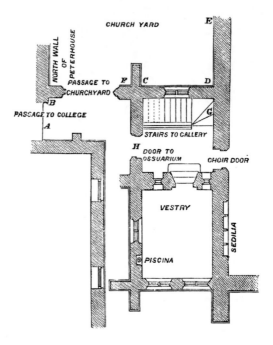

Fig. 18. Ground Plan of Vestry, etc. S. Mary's the Less.

the door leading into the vestry had also been.] The floor of the vestry is raised upon a vault which is used as an ossuarium. This vestry had a narrow escape in 1742, when it was resolved by the College (Ap. 30) that

[1] [" Orb " is a blank window or panel. It is derived from the Latin *orbus*, through the Norman-French *orbe*. See Prof. Willis' Architectural Nomenclature of the Middle Ages, § 78.]

"The Vestry adjoining to the Church be taken down; provided the Consent of the Ordinary and Parishioners be obtained, and that the same can be effected at a reasonable expense, which is left to the judgment of the Master with the Deans and Bursar."

This was not carried out. The reason for it was to clear the space between the Church and Burrough's building, then just finished, as related in Chapter V.

There were several chantries attached to this church. In 1325—6 (19 Ed. II.), the King gave license to Robert de Combreton to grant 3 messuages and 4 acres of land in Cambridge to maintain a chaplain to celebrate daily for the repose of the souls of himself, of his wife Emma, and of his relations, at the altar of the Blessed Virgin in the parish church of S. Peter "extra Trumpeton Gate[1]."

The records of Pembroke College record that a chantry was founded in this church (22 Edw. III. 1348—9) by John Cotton[2]. Part of the site of that College included a tenement belonging to it: and it is the only chantry returned by the Commissioners of Henry VIII. as appertaining to the church we are considering[3]. It is perhaps the same as that previously mentioned, with some confusion in spelling the founder's name, and between the dates of the different muniments and licenses of the foundation.

In 1436 Thomas Lane, Master of Peterhouse (1431—73), bequeathed estates to found a chantry with a chaplain "to celebrate daily *in the new chapel on the north part* of the parish church" for the repose of his soul[4]: and in 1443 the altar of the chantry chapel of Mr Thomas Lane was consecrated in honour of the Annunciation of the Blessed Virgin, and Saint Margaret[5].

The Peterhouse register has also a list of articles " pertaining to the chapel of Henry Horneby [Master (1509—17)] in the

---

[1] MSS. Baker, xxxviii. 149.

[2] Ibid. vii. 179, xvii. 133.

[3] Commiss. Doc^ts. i. 278.

[4] [Peterhouse Treasury, "Collegium" Box A. 8. He directs that his chaplain "continue celebret in nova Capella ex parte boriali ecclesie parochialis predicte et specialiter oret pro animâ meâ." The deed is dated 30 July, 6 Edward IV. (1466). A note in the Register, 82, gives a list of service-books and vestments bequeathed by him "ad celebrandum in Capella Sancte Marie situata in cimiterio ex parte orientali Ecclesie annexe Collegio."]

[5] Register, 83.

Cemetery of S. Mary outside Trumpington Gates[1];" and it is also said that he gave in 1516 many things to be used in the service of this chapel. We may assign Lane's chantry to the north chapel already described, and Horneby's to the opposite chapel.

It is also recorded that on May 4, 1443, two altars were consecrated in the nave of the Church of this College, one on the north to S. Mary Magdalen and S. Margaret, the other on the south to S. John the Evangelist, at the same time that Lane's chantry was consecrated[2]. These altars must have stood, as was very usual, one on each side of the door of the rood-screen, and served for the parish masses, and perhaps for the priest of Cotton's chantry.

In 1446 the executors of John Holbrook, Master (1418—31), made the pavement of the choir and the desks[3], and Mr Leedes built the south porch[4].

On May 28th, 1498, John Warkworth, Master (1473—1500), desired by will that his body, wherever he might happen to die, should be buried in his chapel on the south part of the nave of this parish church. He also bequeathed certain sums for exequies and masses for his soul[5]. He died in 1500. Previously to this Bishop Alcock of Ely had, on Oct. 13th, 1487, consecrated gratis the chapel of Mr John Warkworth in honour of S. Etheldreda, S. Leonard, S. John the Evangelist, S. Mary, and All Saints. The chapel, therefore, was fully completed in his lifetime, and it remains to discover its position. It is stated above to be on the south side of the nave, but in Bishop Bourchier's Register[6] it happens to be recorded that the resignation of a certain John Grove, fellow of the College, took place on Dec. 20,

---

[1] [Register, 100, copied MSS. Cole, xlii. 44.]

[2] Register, 83.

[3] [Ibid.: "Anno domini 1446 in mense Junii Executores recolende memorie Magistri Johannis Holbroke fecerunt fieri pro anime sue memoriali perhenni pauimentum chori cum descis inferiorum gradum sumptibus et expensis suis. Excepto quod collegium exhibebat meremium et lapides in gradibus sacerdotis, diaconi, et subdiaconi, wulgariter vocat' freeston."]

[4] He was bursar of Peterhouse in 1447.

[5] [Register, 103. The original is in the Treasury of Peterhouse, "Collegium" Box, N°. 9. The words are, "in capella mea ex parte australi navis ecclesie parochialis beate marie extra Trumpyngton Gates."]

[6] MSS. Cole, xxv. 27.

1453, in "a certain Chapel dedicated to All Saints next the Chancel of the parish church of S. Mary near the gate." The word *navis* in Warkworth's will must therefore be taken as a general term for the body of the edifice, and there will be no reason to doubt the evidence of the list of Benefactors to Peterhouse, which records that John Warkworth "built the Chapel next to the Church of S. Mary which is now termed the vestry."

In fine, it appears that in 1340 the church of S. Peter was unfit for divine service from the repairs and rebuilding rendered necessary by its ruinous state, so that the scholars had recourse to a private oratory in college. In 1352 the chancel of S. Peter was fit for service and the scholars have license to employ a portable altar there until the new chancel is finished. The word "chancel" is often applied to any chapel, so that it must be considered that some part of the old church was by that time roofed in, and found to be more convenient than the temporary oratory. The present church was dedicated in 1352, and the name changed from S. Peter to S. Mary.

In the middle of the fifteenth century, when the College buildings were being carried on, the Church was also undergoing repairs and refittings, as we gather from the consecration of the altars of the rood-screen in 1443, the pavement and desks of the choir in 1446, and the building of the south porch about 1447. To this period we may assign the perpendicular window and work at the west end next to the porch. The building of the vestry follows about 1485, or rather the completion of it. The work of the gallery bridge and the chambers next to it is also, by style, a part of the fifteenth century work; but, as I have already said, cannot be exactly fixed in date. The similar gallery and gateway at Corpus were built about 1487.

[In 1550—1 a workman was employed to destroy the altars in the choir and little chapel, by which Warkworth's chapel may possibly be meant[1].

Dowsing visited the Church in 1643, and records that

"We brake down 60 superstitious pictures, some popes and crucifixes, with God the Father sitting in a chair and holding a globe in his hand[2]."]

[1] [1550—1. "Et de xij d. Thome Brine pro diruendis aris chori et parvi sacelli."]
[2] Carter's Cambridgeshire, 40.

Cole has left a long description of this Church, dated 28 March, 1743, from which the following portion may be quoted :

"The present Church of Little S[t] Maries as it is always called to distinguish it from that of Great S[t] Maries, or S[t] Mary ad Forum or near y[e] Market consists only of a noble large Nave or Body, but divided ab[t] y[e] middle by a neat Screen, w[ch] runs quite across and so makes a Chancel and Nave, w[ch] is tiled and roofd Archwise with large Arches of wood work w[ch] are handsomely adorn'd wth carv'd work over y[e] part w[ch] constitutes y[e] Chancel.... There are stalls w[ch] run round y[e] Chancel part, to y[e] lowermost step of y[e] Altar, w[ch] stands on an Eminence of two, and rail'd round y[e] uppermost Step. The upper end of it is also beautifully wainscoted and painted from y[e] end of y[e] Stalls on both sides and y[e] E. Wall behind y[e] Altar; y[e] Pannel behind w[ch] immediately is painted of a fine blew and gilt : above w[ch] is also gilt and carv'd I.H.S, and over this a Globe, and on it a large gilt Cross.... Over y[e] Door of y[e] Screen pretty high hangs y[e] Arms of y[e] present Royal Family neatly painted, and was y[e] Gift of M[r] Valentine Ritz, a German Painter who has lived in this Parish near 50 years, and is now very old: he was formerly no indifferent Copier; but now past his Work[1]."]

The roof of the chancel is Jacobean in style, and that of the nave older[2]. But the whole is now condemned as rotten and past repair, and a new roof designed by Mr Scott is ordered to be substituted[3]. The screen was probably cut down to the level of the pews, and the stalls removed, when the present Italian altar-piece and the pews were set up, which appear to belong to the last century and were perhaps part of a "beautification" that took place in 1741.

[When this altar-piece was taken away, three sedilia and a piscina at the east end of the south side were discovered (B, C, D, A, fig. 17), and also an ambry on the north side. Various fragments of clunch and alabaster, painted and gilt, were also found behind it. This led to further investigation, and a niche on each side of the east window was laid open,

---

[1] MSS. Cole, ii. 49. [Valentine Ritts painted the picture of Sir I. Newton in Trin. Coll. Hall.]

[2] [To this statement Professor Willis appends a note of interrogation.]

[3] [A good view of the interior with the roof in question by F. Mackenzie is given by Le Keux, ii. p. 201, and of the east window (exterior) in the Cambridge Portfolio, ii. 489. The following entry in the Catharine Hall accounts for 1646—7, "Giuen to Peterhouse towards the reparation of Little S. Marys . 2 . 0 . 0," indicates some extensive work at that time.]

previously concealed by a monumental tablet, to receive which the tabernacle work had been cut off level with the wall. These niches have been carefully restored, and the pieces found behind the woodwork fitted into their places wherever it was found practicable to do so. The exact size of the original altar was also discovered, by the marks on the eastern wall from which it had been broken down. The present table represents it exactly in width, but is 6 inches lower. The steps also (fig. 17) follow the ancient indications. The whole of this work was executed under the direction of G. G. Scott, Esq., Jun., who also designed the new altar-piece in 1876.]

On the outside of the east end are two tabernacles, now in a hopeless state of dilapidation, placed one on each side of the east window, rising considerably above the level of its present sill. The base of a third, exactly the same in form as the others, is placed in the middle, and once doubtless rose as high as they do, and was connected with the tracery of the window and with the lateral tabernacles by screen-work and other curious devices, which, falling into decay, were all swept away. [A restoration of these was contemplated in 1857, but they were found to be too ruinous, and the idea was wisely abandoned[1]. It is said that they once contained statues of our Saviour, the Blessed Virgin, and S. Peter.]

A restoration of the east window, at an expense of £13, is recorded in the Bursar's Roll for 1639—40. [It was again repaired in 1821[2].]

---

[1] [College Order, Nov. 11, 1857: "That Mr. G. G. Scott be consulted upon the best mode of restoring the East Front of Little S. Mary's Church, and that the niches be measured and models of them taken under his directions with a view to their being restored."]

[2] [June 30, 1821. "Agreed that the East Window of the Chancel in S. Mary's Church be repaired forthwith."]

CHAPTER VIII.

HISTORY OF PARTICULAR BUILDINGS.

Hall.   Combination Room.   Master's Lodge.

HAVING now traced the general architectural history of the College to the present time, we must examine the changes in the principal offices.

HALL.—Of this it is recorded that £4. 15s. 8d. were expended upon the framed screen at the lower end in 1638[1]. In 1705[2] Dr Battell and other contributors gave money, about £40 in all, towards ornamenting the common Hall, which marks the date of its present[3] interior fittings. The exterior next the court was ashlared, with Italian window-dressings, at the same time with the rest of the buildings in 1755; and it was new-roofed in 1791[4].

[In 1868 (Aug. 7), it was decided to restore the Hall, under the direction of Sir G. G. Scott. Loggan's view shews two windows in the body of the Hall, with one, considerably longer, at the east end, opposite the dais. Successive alterations had, however, so completely obscured these details, that a reproduction of them would have been equivalent to a new construction. The architect, in consequence, felt justified in building an oriel

---

[1] "Pro lignis et opere in tabulationem septi in inferiori parte Aule." Bursar's Roll, 1638—9.

[2] College Order, April 23, 1791.

[3] [Prof. Willis wrote this in 1856.]

[4] College Order, April 23, 1791...."that the part of the Estimate given in by Humfreys and Bradwell for necessary Repairs be adopted and likewise that the East side of the Library building next the court be plaistered and the end next the street pointed; and that the Hall be new roofed.—Ordered at the same time that five guineas be given to the Parish towards defraying the expence of rebuilding the Church wall."

towards the court, and in adding five buttresses on that side, and four on the south side, to the hall and buttery, to support, as far as the former building was concerned, the weight of the oak roof which he had designed. The windows on the south side were left, as far as was practicable, in the condition in which they were found. They are of late fifteenth century work. Originally the sills appear to have been not more than four feet above the surface of the ground, as may be seen in the western-most bay on the south side, where the opening has been filled in with brick above a line in the ashlar which marks the former level. The original sill has been preserved. Evidence of the old fourteenth century windows was also found on the north side, and still exists behind the panelling. The panel work of the interior, including the screen and dais, was executed under the direction of the architect by Messrs Rattee and Kett. The whole was completed by February, 1871, at a cost of £7156. 9s. 3d.]

COMBINATION ROOM.—[Cole has left such a precise account of this room as it was arranged in his time that it is printed entire.]

"This curious old Room joins immediately to the East End of the common Hall or Refectory, and is a ground Floor called, The Stone Parlour, on the South Side of the Quadrangle, between the said Hall and the Master's old Lodge. It is a large Room and wainscoted with small oblong Pannels, the two upper Rows of which are filled with Paintings on Board of several of the older Masters and Benefactors to the College. Each Picture has an Inscription in the Corner, and on a separate long Pannel under each much ornamented with painting, is a Latin Distic. I was very desirous of preserving this laudable and very curious, and almost singular Peice of Antiquity in our University; not only out of Regard to the Things themselves; which surely in a religious Society ought to be preserved; but because the Room is now deserted; the Fellows meeting after Dinner in an upper Room above it; so that this Room is going to a visible Decay: Upon this Account I prevailed with my Friend Mr Erasmus Earle formerly Fellow Commoner of Pembroke and since made a Fellow of this College, and also Fellow of the Antiquary Society, to take an exact List of them for me with their Inscriptions and Distics: which he accordingly did for me. And this I am very glad was done at that Time; since which, as I am informed by the present worthy Master [Dr Keene, 1748—56], the right rev: the Lord Bp. of Chester, they have been all taken out of their Pannels, and, as the Bp. told me, he has new framed them and hung them up in his Lodge. The Pictures are ranged all round the Room, and begin at the North Corner of the East Side.

1. A View of the two antient Hostles of the Brothers of Penance, and of Jesus Christ: on the Spot where they stood, Hugh de Balsham Bp. of Ely founded this College in 1280.

Hæc bina fuerunt Scholasticorum Hospitia, in quæ
Fratres Seculares extra Hospitale Divi Johannis traduce-
bantur, quorum Loco hoc Collegium est ædificatum.

Qua præit Oxonium Cancestria longa Vetustas,
Primitus a Petri dicitur orsa Domo.

2. King Edward the First in his Robes, Crown and Cap, a Globe in his left Hand, and a Sword in his Right, with a Profile Face, and the Arms of England by him.

Edwardus Rex Angliæ ejus Nominis primus,
Licentiam dedit fundandi hoc Collegium,
A: D: 1283.

Omnia dum curat Princeps, non ultima Cura est,
Si pius est, Artes sustinuisse bonas.

3. Hugh de Balsham in his Episcopal Robes, Mitre, pastoral Staff in his right Hand and a Book in his Left, with these Arms by him; Gules 3 Crowns Or, for the See of Ely, impaling Gules 2 Keys in Saltire Or; being designed possibly for those of St. Peter.

Hugo de Balsam decimus Episcopus Eliensis, primus
Fundator Collegii Anno Dom: 1284.

Utere Divitiis si te Fortuna bearit,
Hac Iter ad Cœlum est, sic tibi Dives eris.

4. Simon de Montacute Bp. of Ely in his Episcopal Robes, Mitre and Crosier: See of Ely impales Argent, a Fess lozengée Gules, a Bordure Barry Vert and Or for Montacute.

Simon Montis-acuti decimus septimus Episcopus
Eliensis Anno Dom: 1344.

Lex ubi pulsa silet, regnat pro Lege Libido;
Jusque Pudorque ruunt, mox ruitura magis.

5. *Simon Langham Episcopus Eliensis*
Anno Dom: 1395.

The See of Ely impales Gules 2 Keys en Saltire Or. But these are not Bp. Langham's Arms: neither is the Date in Mr Earle's Account just: for Bp. Langham succeeded to Ely 1361, removed to Canterbury five years after, and died at Avignon in 1376. He is habited as a Bishop.

Laus Pueris, Doctrina, Decus florentibus Annis,
Solamen Senio, Perfugiumque Malis.

6. Thomas de Castro-Bernard in a clerical Habit, holding an open Book.

Thomas de Castro-Bernard fuit Magister
Collegii Anno Dom: 1420.

Omnibus impendas ultro, tibi Nemo rependat,
Non Hominis vox hæc, sic jubet ipse Deus.

7. John Holbroke Master in 1430, in a clerical Habit, holding a Book in his right Hand and a Roll in his Left.

Johannes Holbroke Magister Collegii
Anno Dom: 1430.

Partus dant similes Usura, et Vipera fœta,
Qui juvat afflictos, fœnerat ille Deo.

8. Thomas Lane Master 1472, in a clerical Habit, holding a Book with both his Hands.

Thomas Lane Magister Collegii
Anno Dom: 1472.

Fælix Centurio Synagogæ Conditor olim :
Nam Deus huic charus, charus et ipse Deo.

9. John Warkeworth Master in 1498, in a clerical Habit, holding an open Book with both his Hands.

Johannes Warkeworthe Magister Collegii
Anno Dom: 1498.

Dives adoptata gaudeto Prole; probatos
Non cuicunque libet, progenuisse licet.

10. Thomas Denman Master in 1500; in a Doctor of Physic's Robes, with a Book in his right Hand and an Urn in his Left.

Thomas Denman Doctor Artis Medicinæ
Magister Collegii Anno Dom: 1500.

11. Henry Hornbie Master in 1516, in a clerical Habit, with an open Book in both his Hands.

Henricus Hornbie Magister Collegii
Anno Dom: 1516.

Christus laudetur Mundus ne Cornua tollat,
Tollentur justis Cornua nulla malis.

12. Edmund Hanson, D.D., in Doctor of Divinity's Robes, with a shut Book in both his Hands.

Edmundus Hanson Doctor Theologiæ
Anno Dom: 1516.

Pectoribus Scopulos Marmorque evellite prudens,
Qui se stravit Humi, succubuitque Deo.

13. Mr Lownde D. D. in Doctor's Robes, and holding an open Book with both his Hands.

> *Magister Lownde, Doctor Theoligiæ [sic]*
> *Socius Collegii Anno Dom:* 1519.
>
> > Ite procul Zoilus, Momusque et livida Turba,
> > Et vos Frons, Oculus, Lingua superba procul.

14. William Martin, Priest and Fellow of the College, in sacerdotal Robes, and a closed Book in both his Hands.

> *Magister Willelmus Martin, Sacerdos*
> *& Socius Collegii Anno Dom:* 1519.
>
> > Qui Dominum metuit, Divinaque Jussa capessit,
> > Filius ille Dei, & Filius ejus erit.

15. Thomas Burgoygne Master in 1520, in his Doctor's Robes, and holding a closed Book with both his Hands. These Arms by him. Vert a Lion salient Or, impales Argent a Fess Sab: in Cheif 3 Crows and in Base a Cheuron Sable. But these Arms are either painted falsely or so taken; for the Arms of Burgoyne are Azure a Talbot passant; and the impaled Coat, no doubt, was designed for this Master's Mother Margaret the Wife of John Burgoyne of Impington near Cambrige, whose Arms on Brass are twice on her Monument in that Church impaled by those of her Husband as above, viz: a Talbot passant impales a Fess and in Cheif 3 Leopards' Faces and in Base a Cheuron[1].

> *Thomas Burgen Doct: Theol: Magister*
> *Collegii Anno Dom:* 1520.

16. John Edmondes Master in 1527, in Doctor's Robes and holding a closed Book with both his Hands.

> *Johannes Edmondes, Doct: Theol: Magister*
> *Collegii Anno Dom:* 1527.
>
> > Τῶν ἱερῶν ἄγνοια γραφῶν μερόπεσσι βροτοῖσι
> > Μοῦνον ξυμπάντων αἴτιον ἐστι κακῶν.

17. Doctor Shirton Master of Pembroke Hall, in his Doctor's Robes and holding a Book closed in his left Hand and a Roll in his Right, with these Arms by him; viz: Pembroke Hall impaling Party per Fess, Or in the Cheif Part, and in the Base Part, Paly of 4 nebulé, ...and Gules, in Cheif a Label of 3 Points Vert.

> *Doctor Shirton Magister Aulæ*
> *Penbrokiæ [sic] Anno Dom:* 1530.
>
> > Proximus ille Deo, qui paret recte monenti;
> > Dignus et ille Deo qui sibi recta cavet.

---

[1] [For these arms Cole refers to his Fourth Volume, p. 89.]

18.   The Widow of Mr Wolfe, in Widow's Weeds, holding an open Book in both Hands.

Vidua Magistri Wolfe Anno Dom : 1540.

Mortalem Tabithæ Pietas bis vivere Vitam,
Cœlestem Viduæ perpetuamque dedit.

19.   Andrew Perne Master, in his Doctor's Robes, and holding a closed Book in both his Hands: by him are his Arms, viz : Or, on a Cheuron between 3 Pelicans Heads erased Azure, 3 Mullets of the Field: and this Motto ; ΑΛΗΘΕΟΝΤΕΣ ΔΕΝ' ΑΓΑΤΗ [*sic*].

Bibliothecæ Libri Redditus pulcherrima Dona,
Perne, pium Musis te, Philomuse, probant.

Andreas Perne, Doctor Theol: Decanus
Ecclesiæ Eliensis, Magister Collegii, obiit
26 Aprilis Anno Dom: 1573 [*sic*].

20.   Sir Edward North.   He has a golden Chain round his Neck and a Flower in his left Hand, with these Arms by him : Azure, a Lion passant, Or, inter 3 Fleurs de Lis, Argent, for North ; impales, Sab : on a Cheuron embattled inter 3 Eaglets displayed Argent, 3 Trefoils slipped, vert.   This last Bearing is wrong taken or falsely painted ; for on Sir Edw : North's Tomb in Kirtling Church, they are Quaterfoils[1].

Dominus Edoardus North Anno Dom: 1564.

Nobilis hic vere, vere si nobilis ullus,
Qui sibi Principium Nobilitatis erat.

21.   Robert Smith, Scholar of the House, in Robes turned up with Ermine, in a Ruff and a Roll in his left Hand.

Robertus Smith quondam Scholaris
hujus Collegii obiit Anno Dom: 1565.

Dulcia Musarum qui Pauper Tecta reliqui,
Nunc Dives, studiis, consulo, Musa, tuis.

22.   Archbishop Whitgift in the Robes of a Doctor in Divinity and holding a Book closed in his Hands.

Doctor Whitgift quondam Socius
Collegii Anno Dom: 1569.

Quod Paci Whitgifte faves,. Studiisque piorum,
Dat tibi, Pacis amans, candida Dona Deus.

23.   Henry Wilshawe, in a clerical Habit, holding a closed Book in his left Hand.

Henricus Willshawe Doctor[2] Theo
logiæ Anno Dom: 1578.

Quam minime quæris Bona? te doctissime Willshawe,
Vita vel invitum Nobilitate beat.

---

[1] [For these arms Cole refers to his Eighteenth Volume, p. 109.]
[2] [Cole appends in the margin ' sic, in MS. Earle.']

24. Ralph Ainsworth Master in 1644, in his Bachelor of Divinity's Habit, holding a Book closed in his Hands.

Magister Radulphus Ainsworth
Baccalarius [sic] in Theologia, Magister
Collegii Anno Dom: 1644.

25. Robert Slade, in grey Hair, in a Ruff, and holding an open Book in his Hands.

Robertus Slade Ætatis suæ 66,
Anno Dom: 1616.

26. John Blythe, in a Ruff and clerical Habit, holding a Book closed in his Hands.

Johannes Blyihe Baccalaureus
Theologiæ, Socius Collegii An: Ætat:
suæ 57. A: D: 1617.

27. Bernard Hale, Master, in a clerical Habit.

Bernardus Hale S. T. P. Eliensis Ecclesiæ
tum Canonicus, tum Archidiaconus, hujus
Collegii Custos, obiit Anno Dom: 1663.

28. Bishop Cosins, in his Episcopal Robes, without any inscription.

29. Joseph Beaumont, Master of the College, in his Doctor of Divinity's Robes.

Josephus Beaumont S. T. P. Regius, Eliensis
Ecclesiæ Canonicus, atque hujus Collegii Custos
obiit 23. Novembris 1699.

30. Charles Beaumont in his Doctor of Divinity's Robes.

Carolus Beaumont S. T. P. Collegii Socius, magni
illius Beaumonti Filius, obiit 13 Martii 1726[1]."

[This description shews that the room is the same as the present one, or rather, as its western portion : for it originally extended no farther than the point marked O (fig. 2) and was

---

[1] MSS. Cole, xxxv. 112. Carter's Cambridge, 33, but inaccurately. Blomefield (Collectanea, 158) gives the last pictures of the series rather differently :

"24. Robert Slade, aetatis suae 66, 1616.
25. Johannes Blithe, Bac. Theol. Socius Collegii An°. 1617.
26. Magister Radulphus Ainsworth, Bac. Theol. Magister Collegii An°. 1644.
27. Bernardus Hale S.T.P. Eliensis Ecclesiae tum Canonicus, tum Archidiaconus, hujus Collegii custos, obiit An°. 1665.
28. Josephus Beaumont S. T. P. Regius, Eliensis Ecclesiae Canonicus, atque hujus Collegii Custos, obiit 23 Nov. 1699.
29. Thomas Richardson S. T. P.
30. John Whalley, D.D. Regius Professor, is the present Master, 1745."

just 22 feet long.   It was more than doubled in size, as the plan
shews, during the repairs above recorded (1868—70), by the
addition of a set of chambers to the east, and of an oriel to the
south.   The stone fireplace in the west wall was then discovered
behind the wainscot.   It is entirely original with the exception
of some moldings which had been cut off when the panelling
was put up in front of it, and is probably the fireplace of which
the painting has been already recorded in the Bursars' Rolls.
The oak panelling and furniture, designed by Mr G. G. Scott, was
executed by Messrs Rattee and Kett.   The whole effect is now
singularly harmonious and appropriate.   There is no record to
tell us when the wainscot was originally set up.   It is probable,
however, that it would be at about the same time as that of
the Hall.   It was clearly a practice in this College, as Fuller
says, to paint the picture of a distinguished member, with appropriate verses, which apparently were written under a portrait
which had been already hung up, after the death of the person
so commemorated.   In Dr Perne's case the writing of the verses
alone is mentioned in the accounts for 1593—4.   They apparently did not give satisfaction, for they were rewritten in
the same year, and the picture was "refreshed," shewing that it
had been painted some time previous.   In 1616—7 nine shillings
are paid to John Newton the painter for his work about the
verses written under the picture of Mr Slade[1].   The original
panelling had probably been removed at the same time as the
pictures, for that which was taken down as recorded above was
not older than the middle of the last century.   It has been placed
in another apartment in the College[2].   Most of these pictures
have now been brought back from the Master's Lodge, and
have been hung in the Hall, with the Latin distichs restored
according to Cole's record of them.

  In 1868 the stucco was stripped off the south wall of this

---

  [1] [Fuller, p. 73, gives Slade's distich in the following words: " Haeredem voluit
Sladus conscribere Petrum, Clauderet extremum ne sine prole diem."]

  [2] [This conclusion respecting the age of the wainscot, which was arrived at by Mr
G. G. Scott, is confirmed by a passage in the Cambridge Guide for 1799.   "There
were various other Paintings...upon Pannels of wainscot in the old Combination
Room, which upon its being new wainscotted were removed into the Library, where
they remain."]

room and of the Master's chamber above it, and the ancient masonry brought to light. The sash windows were removed, and replaced by others in a suitable style of the fifteenth century. The only addition was the oriel above mentioned, which was continued to the room above. A small vestibule on the west side of the turret (I. fig. 2), by means of which a covered passage was provided into the Hall through a molded doorway of an extremely rich early design, was rebuilt. These works were conducted with so much care for the preservation of every detail that could throw any light upon the past history of the College, that it is easier to trace the architectural history now than before the alterations.]

LODGE.—The Masters continued to occupy the ancient Lodge between the Hall and the Library until the beginning of the last century. But in 1725 (Ap. 29), Dr Charles Beaumont, the son of the Master, Dr Joseph Beaumont, gave by will to the College, to be used as a Lodge, the large and commodious mansion built by himself in 1701 [1], opposite to the College. In 1741, a College order was made "that the House in which the Master now lives be deemed a Legal and Statutable place of Residence for the Master for the time being," as it has continued to be to the present day, the ancient Lodge being converted into chambers.

It appears from the description of Cole quoted above, that the Fellows appropriated the chamber over the old stone Parlour as their Combination Room when the Masters vacated it, for which purpose the turret stair would conveniently adapt it by giving immediate access from the Hall.

[The portion of the College garden immediately adjoining the Lodge was assigned to the Master. Charges respecting it occur frequently in the accounts, among which may be mentioned a repair of the arbour in 1601—2. Its extent is shewn on the plan (fig. 1) from Loggan's map of Cambridge.

A few miscellaneous particulars concerning the College may be briefly noticed. The Clock was put up in 1586—7. The position of this, as we learn from the College order directing its

---

[1] Dyer's Privileges of the University, ii. 19.

removal, was over the Buttery[1]. The seats in the court were repaired in 1589—90: and it was planted with privet in 1600—1, to which hawthorn bushes were added in 1611—12. These are shewn in Loggan's print (fig. 14)[2].]

[1] ["April 2. 1757. Agreed that the Lanthorn over the Butteries be taken down, and the Clock remov'd at as little expense as possible."]

[2] ["1589—90. Et de viij d Swayle reparanti sedilia in Area. 1600—1. Et de xiij d Williams operanti circa ligustrum in area, et de iij d pro radicibus ligustri. 1611—12. circa le quicksett in area."]

CHRONOLOGICAL SUMMARY.

1284. Removal of the Scholars of the Bishop of Ely to two hostels hard by the Church of S. Peter.

1286. Death of the Founder, Bishop Hugh de Balsham: with bequest to his scholars of 300 marks, with which they built a hall.

1307. Acquisition of the site of the Fratres de Pœnitentia.

1352. Dedication of Church of S. Mary the Less.

1374—1417. Repairs are done to Hall and chambers but no other building work.

1424—9. Building on a large scale is being carried on.

1431. Contract for building a Library.

1443. Consecration of the Chantry of Thomas Lane.

1447. Desks and windows of Library made.

1450. Kitchen built.

1460—66. Building of Master's chambers, Combination Room, and chambers.

1487. Consecration of the Chantry of John Warkworth.

1589. Will of Dr Andrew Perne for building a new Library.

1595. Library completed.

1628—32. Chapel built.

1632. Range of Chambers built on north side of entrance court (Dr Richardson's).

1633. South cloister built, and north cloister probably soon after. Elongation to the street of Dr Perne's Library.

1636—40. Issue of letter soliciting subscriptions for these and other works. General repairs of the College undertaken.

1705. Hall wainscoted.

1709—11. North and south cloisters rebuilt by Grumbold.

1725. Dr Charles Beaumont bequeaths his house for a Master's Lodge.

1732—43. New building on north side of entrance court erected by Burrough.

1751. New gates toward the street erected.

1754. Principal court ashlared by Burrough.

1825. Foundation of Gisborne Court.

1848. Considerable repairs done to the College.

1857. Restoration of Church of S. Mary the Less.

1868—70. Restoration of Hall and Combination Room.

APPENDIX.

I. *Deed of Henry III., confirming the Brothers of the Penance in their Site.*

Henricus dei gracia Rex .. Cum dilecti nobis in Christo Prior et fratres de penitencia Jesu Christi quandam aream quam inhabitant prope Burgum nostrum Cantebrig' extra Trumpetone gate ex donacione diuersorum per cartas suas diuersis particulis integratam de nostra licencia sint adepti; nos, pro salute anime nostre ... dictos Priorem et Fratres tanquam ex fundacione nostra ibidem existentes et eciam eorum successores in proteccionem et defensionem nostram suscepimus specialem. Et dimissionem et concessionem quam Johannes Le Rus filius Mauricii Le Rus de Cantebrig' fecit per cartam suam ... de quadam parte aree predicte; Dimissionem...quam Hoellus et Thomas filii Johannis de Berton fecerunt; ... Dimissionem ... quam Magister Thomas filius Walteri de Sancto Edmundo fecit; ... Dimissionem ... quam Josephus Le Bercher fecit; ... Dimissionem ... quam Gilbertus filius Michaelis Herward fecit; ... Dimissionem ... quam Agnes que fuit uxor Johannis de Berton fecit; ... Dimissionem ... quam Henricus Pikerel fecit; ... Dimissionem ... quam Simon filius Johannis de Berton fecit; ... Et Dimissionem ... quam magister et fratres Hospitalis Sancti Johannis de Cantebrig' fecerunt ratas habentes et gratas eas pro nobis et heredibus nostris quantum in nobis est concedimus et confirmamus sicut carte predicte quas dicti Prior et fratres inde habent et quas inspeximus ... testantur. In cuius rei testimonium has literas nostras ... fieri fecimus patentes. Teste meipso apud Wodestoke vicesimo quinto die Junii anno regni nostri quinquagesimo secundo.

II. *Indenture for building the Library.*

Hec indentura facta xii die mensis Februarii Anno regni Regis Henrici Sexti post conquestum nono inter Magistrum Johannem Holbrok magistrum Collegii Sancti Petri Cantebr' et socios eiusdem ex una parte et Johannem Wassyngle de Hynton ex altera testatur quod idem Johannes Wassyngle bene fideliter et sufficienter in fundo et a fundo superius edificabit parietes ostia et fenestras cuiusdam bibliothece edificande in Collegio predicto. Sic videlicet quod omnia· ostia ad dictum opus necessaria et decem fenestras computando duas minores pro una ex bonis lapidibus et durioribus de inferiori lecto lapidicinii philippi Grove citra ultimum diem Aprilis proxime futurum post datum presencium dolabit et complete ad posicionem eorundem formabit.

Necnon dictos parietes citra eundem diem Aprilis edificare incipiet et citra festum quod dicitur Sancti Petri ad vincula ex tunc proxime sequens ad altitudinem decem pedum supra planam terram eriget. Alias insuper fenestras quotcunque ad opus predictum necessarie fuerint citra festum Pasche secundo futurum post datum presencium dolabit et ad posicionem earundem complete aptabit.   Necnon predictas parietes citra festum michaelis Archangeli extunc proxime sequens ad altitudinem aliorum parietum noue fabrice predicti Collegii complete eriget.

Ad quas quidem convenciones bene et fideliter perimplendas idem Johannes Wassyngle se in quadraginta libris obligauit.   Et magister Johannes Holbrok et socii superius nominati solvent Johanni Wassyngle predicto pro dolacione et aptura maioris ostii v. s. vjd : et pro factura cuiuslibet ostii minoris quotcunque fuerint iijs : pro formacione eciam et aptatione cuiuslibet fenestre maioris v. s : et cuiuslibet fenestre minoris ijs. vj.d.   Necnon omni septimana integra quando ipse Johannes Wassyngle infra dictum Collegium super opere predicto operabitur iijs. iiijd, et in septimana non integra secundum ratum et dierum feriatorum numerum.

Dabunt eciam eidem Johanni Wassyngle unam togam de liberata Collegii predicti si in opere predicto bene se gesserit.   In quorum omnium testimonium partes predict' sua sigilla alternatim hiis indenturis apposuerunt.

Dat Cantabr' predict' Anno et die quibus supra.

III. *Building Account of Dr Perne's Library*, 1593.—4.

Et de viis. vjd. pro iili. de le sowder et de xxxs. Graie pro triplici fenestra in le gable ende de le gallery et de iijs. Parkinson scribenti versus Dris Pearne in Conclaui et de iijs. iiijd. famulo mri. Angers pro les extraicts curie Wratting et de iijs. Croslande dealbanti muros bibliothecæ per 3. dies et de ijs. Griffith operanti ibidem per 3. dies et de ixd. pro les heare et de iijs. Croslande pro le beamefillinge le gallery per 3 dies et de iijs. eidem efficienti le halfe pace bibliothecæ et foramina pro les iuistes et de iijs. Cuidam rescribenti versus D : Pearne et picturam reficienti et de vjd. pro charta Dno Pearne scribenti nomina librorum et de ijs. ijd. eidem pro cons' ut patet in billa prefecti et de ijs. viduis Joanes et Scisson purgantibus bibliothecam et de viijd. Crofts pro claue pro cubiculo Dni Pearne et de xls. mro. Duckett custodi bibliothecæ Academiæ pro annua pensione et de vjli. xs. mro. Aercher pro 120 deale boardes et 2 wainscott planckes et de ijs. viijd. Passfeilde pro 4 pillrs. ut patet in billa prefecti et de vs. vijd. pro 26 pedibus de le plancke et 4 stoodes ut patet in eadem billa et de vs. vjd. eidem pro 42 pedibus de le plancke et de vs. eidem pro 60 pedibus de les halfe inche boarde ut patet in eadem billa et de vijs. viijd. pro 36 pedibus de les wainscott plancke et de ijs. p. 2 postibus et de xijd. pro 4 liminibus et de ijd. pro 2 pedibus de les square timber et de vijs. iiijd. pro les nayles et de x^d. ob pro 21 pedibus de les single quarters et de xi^d.$\frac{1}{4}$ pro 15 pedibus de les inche boarde et de ix^s. ix^d. pro les nailes et glewe corde et halfe inche boarde. Et de iii^{li}. x^s. viij^d. Pasfeilde operanti per 53 dies et de lv^s. famulo Pasfeilde operanti per 55 dies et de xxxvj^s. viij^d. puero operanti per 55 dies et de xxix^s. Blackwell operanti per 29 dies et de xij^d. cuidam pro unico die ut patet in eadem billa. Et de xiiij^s. pro vectura de les deale boardes et de xviij^d. les watermen et famulis Pasfeild operantibus circa les deale boardes ut patet in eadem billa et de xj^s. Croftes pro 2 dubble casements pro le ende window in le gallery et de xxj^s. viij^d. pro 13 single casements pro le gallery et de ij^s. iiij^d. eidem aptanti 2 olde casements pro le gallery et de ij^s. pro 2 boultes pro ostio pro le gallery et de iij^{li}. vi^s. viij^d. eidem pro 10 dubble casements pro bibliotheca et de iij^s. eidem pro 100 dicheaded nailes pro ostio et de vi^d. eidem aptanti les hinges et de iij^s. iiij^d. eidem pro pari de les greete hinges et 8 platts pro le shelues et de xvi^d. eidem efficienti 8 platts de supellectile Coll: et de ij^s. iiij^d. eidem pro 10 barres pro supportat^r de les shelues et de xiv^d. pro 2 handles pro les doares et de xij^d. eidem efficienti xl. staples de supellectile collegii et de vij^d. pro xx de les longe spikines et de xiv^d. pro xiv shouldfastes et de xvj^d. pro 2 boultes pro ostio ut patet in eadem billa et de iij^{li}. vj^s. viij^d. Warde pro 140 pedibus glasse pro le gallery et de iij^{li}. xvij^s. vj^d. eidem pro 186 pedibus glasse pro bibliotheca ut patet in eadem billa et de xx^d. Crofts eximenti catenas librorum et de x^s. distributis inter discipulos scribentes nomina librorum bibliothecæ et de v^s. vj^d. Croslande coloranti trabes bibliothecæ et de iiij^s. eidem operanti in cubiculo D^{ni} Pearne et de ij^s. pro les roughe tyles et de vj^d. pro les gronsells et de xij^d. pro coloribus ut patet in eadem billa et de xij^d. Archer pro le frame pro pictura D. Pearne ut patet ibidem.   Et de ij^s. vj^d. viduis Joanes et Scisson verrentibus aream Collegii et de vj^d. Croslande pro xl bricks et de viij^d. eidem pro operario purgante hospitium et de v^s. pro pensione balivi de Wratting et de xv^s. lectori græco.

IV. *Form of Letter soliciting Subscriptions.*

Magister et Socii Collegii Sancti Petri Cantabrig: Salutem in Christo.

Kal. Martij A.D. MDCXXXvj.

Ingens jam diu tenuit Petrenses Tuos desiderium ut venerandum istud et Primipilare Collegium senio suo pene confectum novo splendescat cultu.   Religiosa vere cura est, quæ publicis literarum Pietatisque monumentis impenditur.

Cœpimus a Sacris, ac quod summâ animorum gratitudine agnoscimus, tandem in Domo S^{ti} Petri exstructa est Domus Dei, nec illa invenusta, sed nec ornata satis nec absoluta.

Perreximus ad Musea et reliqua Scientiarum Domicilia, ut quæ caduca nuper et prope ruitura videbantur, non sine venustate quâdam sarta tecta posteris relinquamus. Quin ut aucta jam instruatur Bibliotheca, Area insuper et Aula Publica, Musarum Refectoria ne præ cæteris Academiæ Collegiis sordescant, omni quo possumus nixu contendimus. Sed quæ est nostra Infælicitas, post absumptas propriæ tenuitatis vires, post varias aliorum suppetias erogatas (æs alienum a nobis contractum silemus) adeo cœptis hisce Nostris exhaustum est Ærarium, ut nisi nova aliunde succurrat Beneficentia, plane nobis tantis oneribus succumbendum sit.

Supplex hinc (Vir præstantissime) Tibi nunc fit Petrensis Domus, olim Mater Tua, ut siqua apud Te memoria Domus Tuæ, Domus antiquæ, residet, hanc tenuitatem suam tantis conatibus imparem Pietate Tua et Munificentia sublevares. Potuit certe pluribus Benignitatem Tuam ambire, sed apud virum optimum talibusque votis sponte facilem, satis efficax esse solet Rei ipsius dignitas. Quæ tanta est ut quantum ei Gratiæ et Beneficentiæ contuleris, tantum ornamenti Nomini Tuo consequutus fueris, cui nos deditissimos semper habiturus es. Feliciter vale.

V. *Accounts for Fittings in the Chapel*, 1632—35.

Computus novi Sacelli a solenni ipsius Dedicatione Martii 17°. A°. Do. 1632°. ad festum Sancti Michaelis A°. 1633°.

[*Receipts.*]

Et computat de xi li. a Christophero Wren ... et de x li. a magistro Gulielmo Greene in Ornatum Sacelli contributis; et de xij li. ij s. ix d. pro calicibus et operculis argenteis (ex consensu) divenditis; viz: pro calice uno Norimbergico et operculo argenteis ac deauratis (ad unciarum 20 pondus et dim : unciæ) v li. xij s. ix d; et pro alio calice cum duobus operculis (ad 26 unciarum pondus) vj li. x s. et de x li. ix s. ij d. in oblationibus Die consecrationis et de x li. ex oblatione privata; et de iiij li. vij s. in oblationibus in sacra synaxi 4ᵒʳ. diversis anni temporibus et de vij li. iiij s. iij d. in Censu Sacelli a festo Purificationis ad Sancti Michaelis.

Summa lxvˡⁱ. iijˢ. ijᵈ.

[*Payments.*]

Et [computat] de xiij li. v s. in Invitatione Episcopi Eliensis visitoris nostri in Consecrationem Novi Sacelli ... Et ... de xijᵈ. mundanti Sacellum ante consecrationem, et de xxjˢ. iiijᵈ. pro 24. Storeis contractioribus pro Magistro et Sociis (in quas inclinent genua); et pro 10 longioribus in usum communicantium; et de jˢ. ixᵈ. pro duobus Cereis majoribus mensæ Dominicæ; et de xxijˢ. xᵈ. pro 8 libris Liturgiæ Latinæ; et de xxiiijˢ. iiijᵈ. pro 4 aliis libris Anglicanis, Bibliis scil. duobus et duobus Liturgiis vernaculis constringendis et ornandis in usum Sacelli. Et de xiiij^{li}. xix^s. j^d. pro 6 ulnis et amplius Syndonis purpureæ tenuioris, et pro quatuor ulnis coccineæ, ex quibus frontale superius et inferius conficiebantur cum palla mensæ superstrata (omnia xylino panno subtus corroborata); pulvinar etiam oblongum ad Magistri sedem adaptatum cum tribus aliis minoribus, sarcinulis plumeis oppletis cum fimbrialibus suis et nodis angularibus in usum et ornatum mensæ; et pro duobus libris ejusdem serico villoso involutis; et de ix s. ij d. pro fimbrialibus lateralibus et angularibus nodosis pulvinaris quarti in usum suggesti Concionatorii; et de iiij^{li}. ij^s. M^{ro} Cutler pro Salmo suo redditis cujus loco Polubrum dedit et obtulit in usum Sacræ mensæ (ad recipiendas nimirum Oblationes in Eucharistia solenni) argenteum, amplum et perpulcre deauratum cum insignibus ipsius et Collegii incisis. Et de iiij^{li}. xi^s. pro duobus Oenophoris argenteis inaurandis in usum celebrantium; et de iiij^s. vij^d. pro vectura omnium a Londino; et de xlviij^s. pro Pallio sacro in usum ministri Sacra peragentis; et de xxxv^s. vj^d. Ashley, viz: xv^s. pro tribus suggestis et iij^s. pro duobus scabellis, pro mensa vj^s. et v^s. pro tabula supra mensam parieti affixâ et appensâ et duobus scalis vj^s. et de vj^d. pro mundandâ integâ vetustâ; et de vj^d. pro alia matta in Sedem Ministri, et de iij^s. vj^d. pro pulvino sessili ejusdem; et de viij^s. vij^d. pro candelabris minutis æneis in usum Sacelli; et de xij^d. pro suscitabulo ignario; et de v^s. pro exaratione binâ formulæ Consecrationis; et de xij^d. pro libello Inventorii apparatus Sacelli; et de v^s. v^d. pro verriculis, scopis, et contis aliisque utensilibus in munditiam Sacelli. Et de iiij^s. iiij^d. fusori Campanario pro duobus itineribus a Walden ad Cantabrigiam ad visendam campanam Horologicam; et de vj^d. Lotrici pallii Sacri; et de xxv^{li}. xvij^s. iiij^d. pro duobus paribus Candelabris argenteis et eleganter auratis in mensam Dominicam; et Calice cum operculo similiter deauratis (pondus Candelabb: calicis, et operculi, 70 unciarum) Et de xij^{li}. uij^s. pro calice consimili et operculo (31 unciarum) Eucharistico.

Summa lxxi^{li}. x^s. ix^d.

1633—34.

Et [computat] de viij li. ix s. iiij d. Magistro Tolly pro peristromatis et de j s. v d Tabellario ea deferenti; et de xxvij d. Rule pro virgis ferreis et uncis...

1634—35.

Et [computat] de xxxvj s Roberto Rule fabro ferrario pro 4 transermis, et de ij s Philippo Blisse easdem pingenti; et de iij s. iiij d. Carbasher vitrum eisdem adaptanti[1].

---

[1] [The words in this and the previous accounts will be explained as far as possible in the Glossary.]

Lightning Source UK Ltd.
Milton Keynes UK

175311UK00001B/15/P